W9-AHH-008

Designing with Light

Designing with Light

Victoria Meyers

Abbeville Press Publishers
New York London

First published in the United States of America in 2006
by Abbeville Press, 137 Varick Street, New York,
NY 10013

First published in Great Britain in 2006 by Laurence
King Publishing Ltd, 71 Great Russell Street, London
WC1B 3BP

Book design: Wayne-William Creative, Inc.

Printed and bound in China.

First edition
10 9 8 7 6 5 4 3 2 1

Library of Congress Cataloging-in-Publication Data

Meyers, Victoria.
Designing with light / by Victoria Meyers.– 1st ed.
p. cm.
Includes bibliographical references.
ISBN 0-7892-0880-6 (alk. paper)
1. Light in architecture. 2. Daylighting. 3. Lighting, Architectural and decorative. I. Title.

NA2794.M49 2006
729'.28–dc22
2005032605

For bulk and premium sales and for text adoption procedures, write to Customer Service Manager, Abbeville Press, 137 Varick Street, New York, NY 10013 or call 1-800-ARTBOOK.

Front cover: hanrahanMeyers architects,
White Space residence, New York (see p. 66)
Back cover: Steven Holl Architects, Sarphatistraat
Offices, Amsterdam (see p. 119)
Page 2: hanrahanMeyers architects,
White Space residence, New York (see p. 79)

Designing with Light
A Cross-Disciplinary Approach
Page 8

Architecture and Light
Page 20

Color
Page 22

Lines
Page 34

Form
Page 48

Glass
Page 60

Windows
Page 80

Sky Frames
Page 94

Shadows
Page 104

Reflection
Page 118

Designing with light is an intimidating endeavor for most, even though the examples collected in this volume make it seem almost effortless. "So what we're aiming for isn't greater intensity of light... Not 'More light!' but 'More colored light!' should be our motto," wrote Paul Scheerbart in 1914 in his *Glasarchitektur*. The designers and artists featured in this book indeed know how to modulate light and color and achieve the space Scheerbart dreamt of, an architecture of fields, rather than walls.

Paola Antonelli
Curator, Department of Architecture and Design
Museum of Modern Art, New York

The idea that light is a material with a presence seems more scientific than artistic. Light is the set of electromagnetic waves whose frequency lies in the narrow (but visible to the human eye) spectrum of $3.9 \times 10^{14} – 7.5 \times 10^{14}$ Hertz range. But, of course, despite its weightlessness and its general invisibility, light is always deeply significant because it allows us to see and for us to see it. Nature and technology are both illuminated discourses, both uneasy with the obscure. Light is a substance—a continuous force—through which we move as it moves through us. It is mostly an apparition—an appearance that suffuses our existence so completely that we forget it until we see how often we use it in an optimistic language that wants its influence; enlightenment, light music, light humor, light of my life, light my fire, light brigade, light touch, light reading, light hearted, light house, light bulb, making light, the light of reason, shed light on, the speed of light, let there be light. Light is always making waves in our words and our worlds. It is artists who suffuse their work with issues of light. In this book there is still very strong evidence that although artists don't necessarily use northern light in their studios anymore, their concern for the particulars of light burn as ardently bright as ever.

Bruce Ferguson
Dean, Columbia University
School of the Arts
New York

Opposite ▪ Steven Holl Architect, Chapel of St. Ignatius, Seattle, Washington.

Designing with Light

A Cross-Disciplinary Approach

Mary Temple, *Reflection,* acrylic paint on existing interior wall surfaces.

LIGHT

In my practice, hanrahanMeyers architects, we have pursued investigations into light as an area of special interest. Light goes hand-in-hand with architecture, as it does with many of the arts. We have pursued light by developing new window and skylight prototypes, and through the use of color both as a direct and reflected medium in our projects.

This area of interest is directly connected with vision and visuality. Light can create illusions of depth of field. It can create drama, a sense of openness, and a sense of spirituality. Vision is our primary means of reading our world.

We live in an age when 'light' as a concept is challenged as never before. In the eighteenth century, discoveries were made about the refraction of light. At that time it seemed a miracle that something as clear as 'white' light, when bent through the medium of a prism or a raindrop, would yield color. Today our concept of light, along with other natural phenomena, continues to be tested and altered by science.

Einstein's theory of relativity, based on the maximum speed of light in a vacuum, $e = mc^2$, set the standard for scientific and philosophical reflection in the twentieth century. Einstein's theory is based on the premise that nothing can exceed the speed of light, and it made the speed of light the yardstick of modern physics. Although light can be slowed as it travels through various media, nothing can exceed the maximum speed of light. When light beams refract through a raindrop or a prism, for example, the act of slowing the speed of the light creates colors, yielding a rainbow.

Light and the refraction of light has engaged the attention of thinkers such as Aristotle, Pliny, Leonardo, Descartes, Newton, Goethe, and Wittgenstein. Newton's *Opticks* of 1704 was the result of an investigation dating back to antiquity, to Arabic scientists, and to medieval authors such as Al-Hazen, and, later, Bacon, Kepler, and Huygens. Light has always been the source of new concepts in physics.[1]

In the early twentieth century the philosophical ramifications of the theory of relativity also inspired artistic innovations. Its influence is particularly evident in the work of Marcel Duchamp, arguably the most influential artist of the century.

More recently, in her ground-breaking work at Harvard, Lene Hau has slowed the speed of light to 0 miles per hour. No one yet knows the implications this discovery holds for the future of scientific research. What can be surmised, however, is that every aspect of culture, including the arts, will be affected by this development. It is this celebration of 'the new' that is most exciting about light. To study the history of advancement in science and scientific research, is to study the development of theories about light.

Just as 'all roads lead to Rome,' all advances in science, art and architecture lead to light. Relativity led to a new, relativistic set of developments in the arts and in architecture. Now that the speed of light can be controlled, a new world of artistic and cultural interpretations will follow. The architecture of the twenty-first century will incorporate this new milieu of scientific thought and revolution into itself. It is this on-going revolution in thinking that this book attempts to address and chronicle.

THE INSPIRATION OF COLOR AND LIGHT: GOTHIC ARCHITECTURE

Abbot Suger, the Abbot of the Church of St. Denis in the twelfth century, saw color

'White' light when refracted through the medium of a prism yields color.

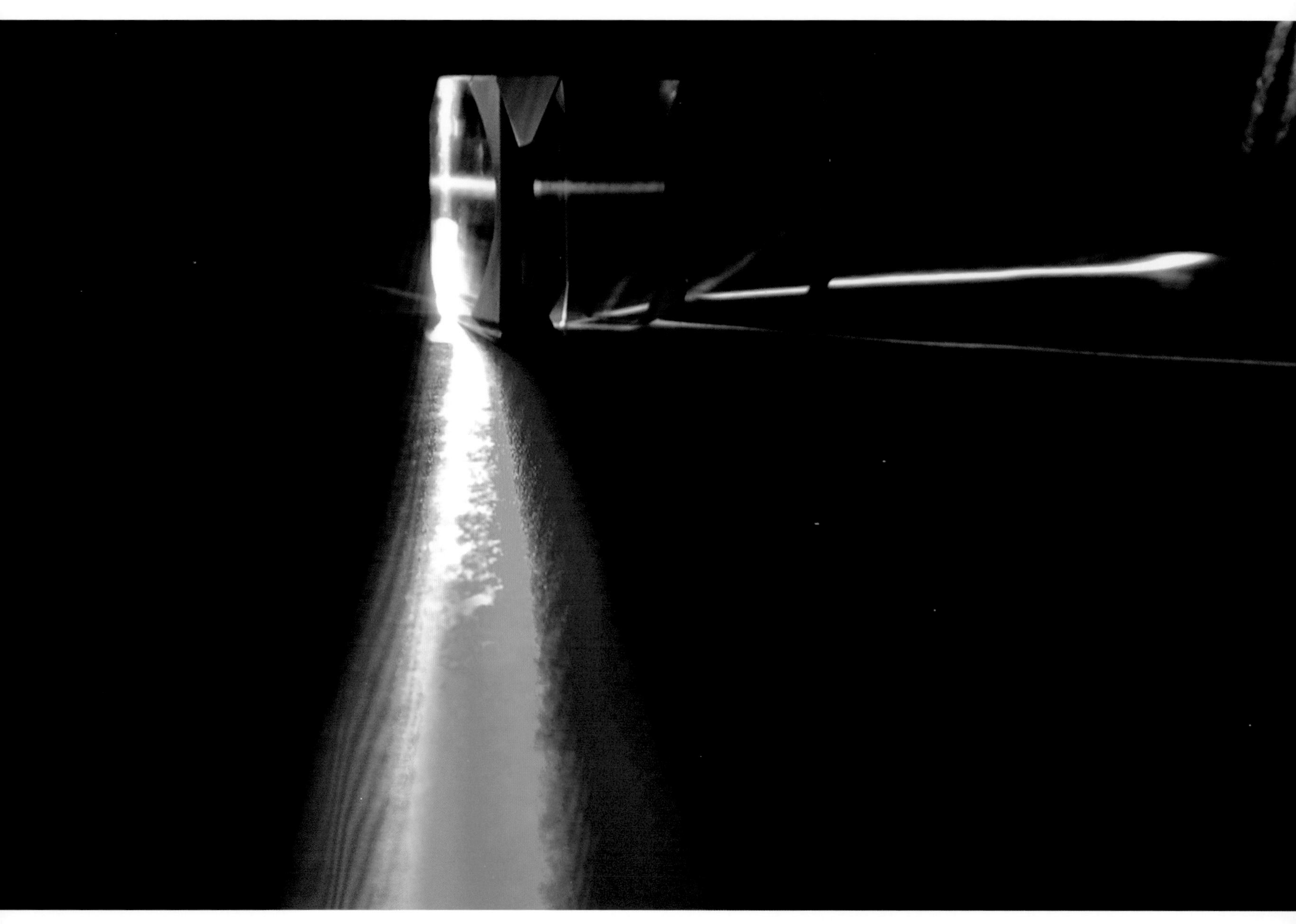

Bill Viola: *Chott el Djerid (A Portrait in Light and Heat)*, 1979. Videotape, color, monosound; 28.00 minutes. Photo: Kira Perov.

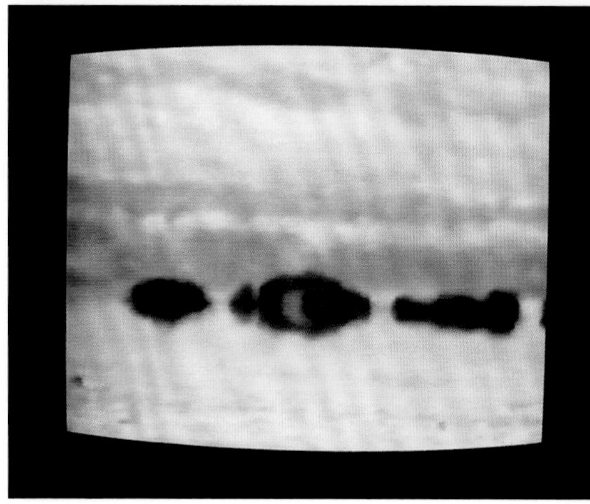

and light as the most important aspects of church design. Suger set about redesigning the abbey church of St. Denis as a reflection of his belief that light and color are the closest representations we have of spirit. When St. Denis was completed in 1144, the Gothic style was born from Suger's search for an architecture of light.

Light continues to be the most inspiring element of architecture, art, music, and life. That inspiration has altered in response to developments in the sciences, reflected in the arts and philosophy of each era.

What follows is a brief survey of contemporary culture, including video art, light art, and sculpture; as well as new developments in science, music and the theater arts. This brief survey attempts to convey the far-reaching effect that ideas concerning light have on contemporary culture. Following this survey, the second half of the book is dedicated to the influence of light on contemporary architectural practice.

VIDEO ART: FILM AND LIGHT

Film and photography are made possible by light. Both art forms originate from early experiments with light, specifically the development of the camera obscura ('dark chamber' into which light is admitted through a double-convex lens, forming an image of external objects) and the camera lucida ('light chamber' wherein the rays of light from an object are reflected by a prism to produce an image). The video installations of Bill Viola are immediate and primitive to the point of allowing viewers to re-enter the space of these original instruments of film.

Viola is widely recognized as a leading video artist on the international scene. His video installations—environments that envelop the viewer in image and sound—employ state-of-the-art technologies and are distinguished by their precision and direct simplicity.

Since 1972 Viola has used video to explore the phenomena of sense perception as an avenue to self-knowledge. His work focuses on universal human experiences: birth, death, and the unfolding of consciousness. It has roots in both Eastern and Western art as well as Islamic Sufism, Christian mysticism, and Zen Buddhism.

Viola has carved a niche as a unique artist working in a new medium. His work is deeply enmeshed in intersecting spiritual traditions, from ancient to contemporary. He has been instrumental in establishing video as a vital form of contemporary art, and has helped to expand its scope in terms of technology, content, and historical reach.

In Viola's installation *Chott el Djerid (A Portrait in Light and Heat)*, desert mirages are set against images of the bleak winter prairies of Illinois and Saskatchewan, Canada.'[2] *Chott el Djerid* is the name of a vast, dry salt lake in the Tunisian Sahara Desert, where mirages often form in the midday sun. Here the intense desert heat manipulates, bends, and distorts light rays to such an extent that you actually see things that are not there. Trees and sand dunes float away from the ground, the edges of mountains and buildings ripple and vibrate, color and form blend into one shimmering dance.

Viola's video deals poetically with the phenomena of light reflection and refraction, recording naturally occurring light distortions. Image number ten (opposite below), cut from the video, shows forms in the desert landscape hovering in the sky.

There is a resemblance between these images and the works of the nineteenth-century Impressionist painters. Both attempt to put the viewer into direct contact with the phenomena of reflected and refracted light. They immerse viewers in the atmosphere of other places through the representation of light.

Viola's *The Veiling* uses beams of light projected toward one another from two directions to create an impression of images moving toward one another. The following text describing *The Vieling* was written by Viola for the Whitney catalog to describe his installation at the Whitney Museum in 1998:

"Thin parallel layers of translucent cloth hang loosely across the center of a dark room. Two projectors at opposite ends of the space face each other and project images into the layers of material. The images show a man and a woman as they approach and move away from the camera, viewed in various nocturnal landscapes. They each appear on separate opposing video channels, and are seen gradually moving from dark areas of shadow into areas of bright light. The cloth material diffuses the light, and the images dissipate in intensity and focus as they penetrate further into the scrim layers, eventually intersecting each other as gossamer presences on the central veil. Recorded independently, the images of the man and the woman never coexist in the same video frame. It is only the light from their images that intermingles in the fabric of the hanging veils. The cone of light emerging from each projector is articulated in space by the layers of material, revealing its presence as a three-dimensional form that moves through and fills the empty space of the room with its translucent mass."[3]

LIGHT ART: THE ART OF LIGHT

How we see is crucial to our perception of art. Beginning with the Renaissance invention of one-point perspective, and through the nineteenth-century fascination

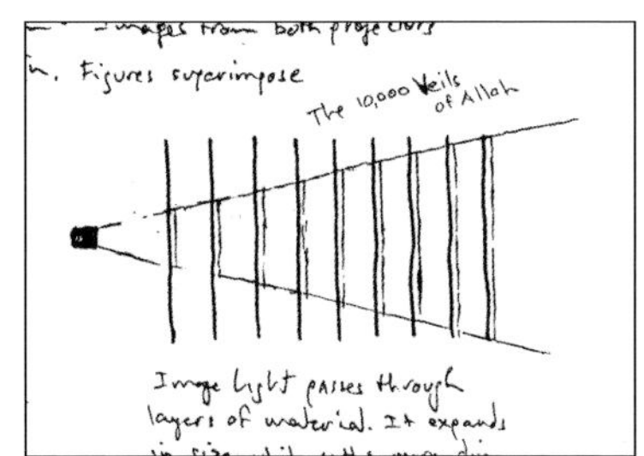

Top left ▪ Central scrim—Images from both projectors meet and align so that figures superimpose.

Left ▪ Receding and advancing figures—the parallel surfaces of the scrims catch the light of the image, which passes through to the deeper scrim layers.

Bottom left ▪ Image light passes through layers of material. It expandss while getting more dim and diffuse. Light from one projector crosses with the other.

Below left and right ▪ Bill Viola, *The Veiling*, 1995. Layers of translucent scrim material can catch and diffuse the light of the images.

Top to bottom right ▪ Dan Flavin, *Untitled*, installation at the Chinati Foundation, Marfa, Texas, 2000. Pink, green, blue and yellow fluorscent light.

Opposite top ▪ Rei Naito, *One Place on the Earth*. Tent installation illuminated by candles.

Opposite bottom ▪ Mary Temple, *Reflection*. Acrylic paint on existing gypsum wall board, wood floor, and carpet.

with light revealed in Impressionist art, to the contemporary era and the proliferation of light art by artists such as James Turrell and Robert Irwin, light is not only the means of illuminating a subject, but becomes the subject itself.

Contemporary light art could be said to date from the 1960s when a number of southern California artists began using fiberglass, cast acrylic, polyester resin, and glass as media for their works. These new atmospheric works presented light as a medium of experience to viewers. Instead of looking at a work of art, the viewer is placed inside it so that the work becomes an experience.

These works blur the boundaries between painting, sculpture, and architecture, making color and light, and their dispersal in space the subject of the art. Particularly relevant to this use of light as a medium for art is the work of Dan Flavin. Born in New York City in 1933, Flavin had his first solo exhibition of assemblages and watercolors in 1961 at the Judson Gallery. The year also marked the beginning of Flavin's use of electric light as a medium for artistic expression. In 1963 Flavin began to work solely with commercially produced fluorescent bulbs with the completion of *the diagonal of personal ecstasy (the diagonal of May 25, 1963)*. For the rest of his career Flavin's medium was fluorescent light.

Flavin's art inverted the typical museum experience of moving from room to room to view pictures. Instead, his installations highlighted the spatial containers where they were displayed. 'The voids... became the means by which he reconceptualized sculpture and space, investing corners, baseboards...in short, every place but that traditionally reserved for the display of art, with a previously unacknowledged presence.'[4]

Richmond Hall is the result of a project commissioned by the Menil Collection in Houston, in 1996. Flavin had been discussing an installation of his work here since 1970.

Built in 1930, Richmond Hall has a simple rectangular shape with a storefront and an open interior reflecting its former life as a grocery store. The main part of the installation is in the large open interior space, 125 feet (38 metres) deep by 50 feet (15 metres) wide. An arrangement of 4-foot (1.2-metre) fixtures extends along the two longer walls. Mounted about 4 feet (1.2 metres) above the floor, running the length of the walls, filtered ultraviolet lights face into the room and separate vertical fluorescent lights. These are offset, the top bulbs facing the back wall of the room, the bottom row facing the front wall. The bulbs alternate in a sequence, of pink, yellow, green and blue.

The central, horizontal ultraviolet light blends the colored lights to form white light. A skylight in the center of the space allows daylight into the room, and gives visitors a tabula rasa, where they can check the coloration of Flavin's mixed light (white light) against daylight.

This piece works with fluorescent light to produce a very similar effect to the composer, Arvo Part's, musical composition, *Für Alina* (see page 15). Both *Richmond Hall* and *Für Alina* blend chromatic scales of light to produce a mixture, yielding white light.

Flavin was associated with other artists of the Minimalist school, including Carl Andre, Donald Judd, and Robert Morris. It was through his close friendship with Donald Judd that Flavin's most recent installation was planned and finally executed at the Chinati Foundation in Marfa, Texas in 2000. The installation consists of interior lighting with fluorescent lights of six barrack buildings at the Chinati Foundation, a former military base. The six buildings are planned in an alternating scheme. Two fixtures and tubes are always attached back to back, illuminating the space in two opposite directions. The first two buildings glow in pink and green, the following two in blue and yellow, and the last two bring all four colors together to make 'white light.'

Light is also the primary focus of the work of the artist Rei Naito. Her work relates ancient traditions of Japanese culture to new technologies. By constructing environments in a process reminiscent of an Ise Shrine, Naito creates the sensibility of the Ise Shrine, using modern technologies and natural light sources. Her work consists of installations that illuminate with light, almost invisible drawings titled *namenlos/Licht,* and performance/art installations.

Naito's work brings viewers into contact with a unique sense of space and time, and proportion and light. Much like Dan Flavin, Naito develops her installations as holistic environments. Light is a key aspect of each environment, creating the perimeter of the space and the mood of the piece.

One Place on the Earth is Naito's best-known work. In 1997 this piece represented Japan at the Venice Biennale. *One Place on the Earth,* like an Ise Shrine, has been reconstructed many times. The piece was originally shown at Sagacho Exhibit Space in Tokyo in 1991.

In *One Place on the Earth* space is created by a large white tent with a continuous perimeter of glowing candles. The project deals with the physical senses of touch, vision and perception.

The tent for *One Place on the Earth* is a space about perception, elucidation, and the act of seeing and understanding, through light. Naito's tent installations

Right ▪ Lene Hau conducting experiments in manipulating the speed of light.

have clearly defined perimeters, marked by a ring of candles that hold the edge of the space.

The contemporary light artist, Mary Temple, bases her work around light and perception. A particularly interesting aspect of Temple's work is that she studies light by never actually portraying real light. Instead she plays with the viewer's emotional and perceptual relationship to light by painting images of window reflections in windowless rooms.

Temple's work plays with and modifies aspects of environmental perception. Her window sculptures appear as light and shadows cast on a wall from a nearby window. The shadows may be from plant life surrounding the window, or just the geometry of the structure of the window frame. They are comprised of an image of light painted on the wall. The conceptual sculpture created by the viewer lasts for only that moment when she or he is convinced that what they are seeing is actually light and cast shadows.

Speaking about her work, Temple summarizes her relationship to light, art, and architectural space thus: "Imagine a windowless room in which there appears to be strong light raking the wall and pooling onto the floor. The rectangle of light seems to be coming from a nearby window, and as you turn to find the source, you understand the shape, size, and location of the (non-existent) window, as well as the time of day the light references. When painting these site-specific trompe l'oeil installations, I rely on the viewer to complete the architectural intervention by conceptualizing a window. In this work and other recent projects I'm interested in what informs the emotional stability of a site, how tenacious or fragile our memory of an environment is, and how I might affect conceptual modifications to physical places."

PHYSICS AND LIGHT: NEW BREAKTHROUGHS IN SCIENCE

Science and changes in scientific ideas have, through the centuries, been precursors of changing ideas in the arts. Today we are once again in the midst of a scientific revolution through the work of Lene Hau, the physicist who has succeeded in slowing the speed of light to 0 miles per hour.

On February 18, 1999, a paper reporting the results of her experiments on light was published on the cover of the leading scientific journal *Nature*. Hau, the leading author of the paper, with her colleague Steve Harris, and two of her Harvard students, reported the results of their experiment in which a beam of laser light was slowed to the astonishingly low speed of 38 miles (61 kilometres) per hour. By comparison, light in a vacuum travels at about 186,000 miles (299,338 kilometres) per second.

Hau's laboratory at the Rowland Institute for Science in Cambridge studies the interaction of lasers with a matter called Bose-Einstein condensate. By shining precisely tuned lasers on a condensate, or cloud, of ultra-cold sodium atoms, Hau and her team reduced the speed of a light beam to a pace slower than 38 miles (61 kilometres) per hour.

Initially, Hau's group succeeded in reducing the speed of light to 56 feet (17 meters) per second. Most recently, they have stopped a light pulse altogether, parked the pulse in a cold atom cloud, and then controllably revived it. Hau's work on ultra-slow light and atomic-wave guides for cold atoms has forged entirely new paths in optics and nonlinear optics.

This achievement, noted by newspapers, magazines and broadcasters around the world, heralds many new practical applications. These include the development of optical switches that will improve the performance of computers enormously. Recently Hau won a MacArthur Fellowship for her work on stopping light and was appointed to the Royal Danish Academy of Sciences in April 2002.

MUSIC AND LIGHT

Historically, music has been compared to the other arts through musical harmony and proportioning systems. In architecture, from the fifteenth to the eighteenth centuries, the harmonies of the musical scales served as evidence that exact ratios underlay our perceptions of beauty. Since measure was as important in architecture as in music harmonies similar to those found in the musical scale were sought to account for the harmonious disposition of buildings.[5]

Musicians and composers have collaborated with architects and artists throughout history, and there are many examples of the fruits of these discussions. A famous example is the collaboration between the composer Xenakis and the architect Le Corbusier.

The work of three composers who reference light in their musical compositions reverses this relationship of music to the other arts. In this instance, light, which inspires the visual arts, is taken as the inspiration for musical works.

Arvo Part was born on 11 September 1935 in Paide, a town just outside the Estonian capital, Tallinn. Part's *Third Symphony*, premiered in 1971, marked an intermediate step on the way to his mature compositional style, presented for the first time in the 1976 piano piece, *Für Alina*. This system of musical compositional, which Part calls the 'tintinnabuli style', has formed his approach in all works written since then.

Commenting on the 'tintinnabuli style,' Arvo Part explained how his idea for creating musical compositions related to the properties of white light: 'I could compare my music to white light which contains all the colors. Only a prism can divide the colors and make them appear: this prism could be the spirit of the listener.'

The first seminal note Part notated in 1976, after long years of preparation, is the sustained octave in the low bass at the start of the piano piece *Für Alina.* Above it sounds, for the first time, the connection of triadic notes that characterizes his 'tintinnabuli style.' *Für Alina* was one of seven works performed in Tallinn in 1976, at a concert premiering the initial results of the new compositional style.

It is to this period of new departures that the artistic concept of Part's recording, *Für Alina,* harkens back, and it does so through transformation. Part establishes a link between two works in this recording embodying the fundamental traits of the 'tintinnabuli style.' Three interpretations of the duet *Spiegel im Spiegel,* written in 1978, become formal pillars positioned before, between, and after two solo renderings of *Für Alina.*

The title of *Spiegel im Spiegel* (German for 'mirror') is a precise description of what happens in this piece. The part for the stringed instrument is constructed as a mirror. The phrases it plays—each one successively adding one more note of the scale—always return, by steps or jumps, to the mirror axis, the central A. The piano mirrors the violin part twice with pure F-major triads, once at close range above it, but also with a layer of alternately higher and lower pitches recreating on a large scale the narrower tonal space traversed by the violin. The piano also confirms the melody notes of the violin with parallel thirds and octaves. Mirror images allow three further voices to unfold from the core voice.

"I could compare my music to white light which contains all colors."
—Arvo Part

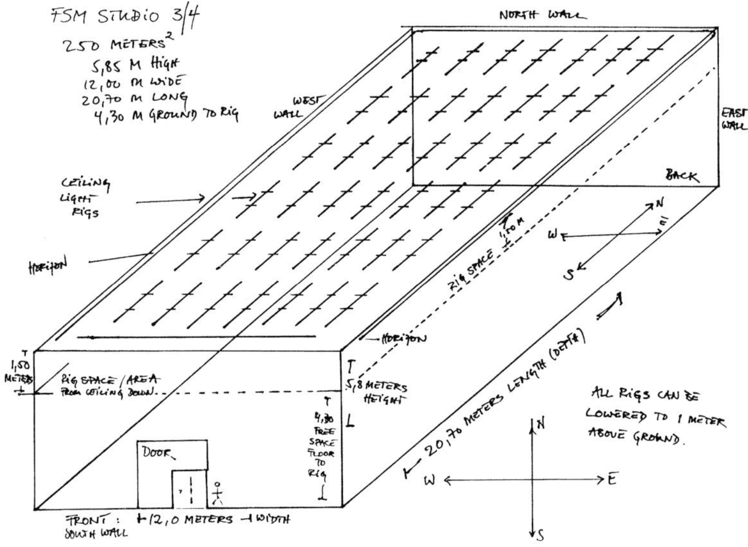

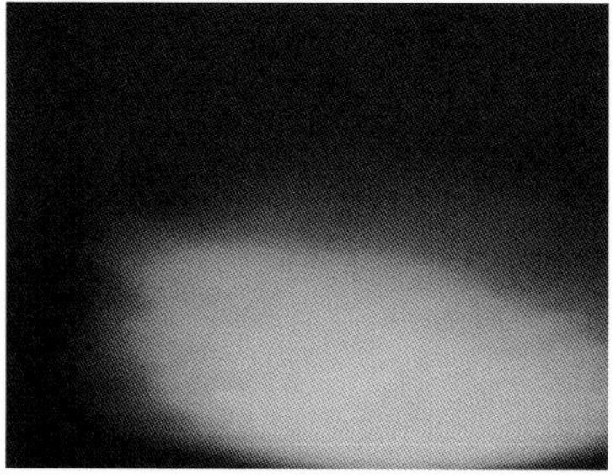

Top ▪ Diagram of the television studio where *One*[11] was filmed.

Above left and right ▪ Film clips from the video *One*[11] produced with the German production company Lohner Ranger, premiered September 19, 1992, in Cologne, Germany.

The CD *Für Alina* is Part's poetic interpretation of white light—using musical chords as representations of various colors of light. These 'colors' are overlaid in the piece and recombined to produce 'white light.'

An optical prism is a simple, regular construction of transparent, light-refracting material, which fulfills its function when two of its surfaces are inclined toward one another at a specific angle. As Part explains: 'A prism acting on white light is the analyzing instrument that separates its constituent rays into their original classes. If the first prism is followed by a second, the 'colorific rays' can be brought together again and so recreate white light.'[6]

Part presents light, broken into constituent colors, that is meant to be recombined, through the interpretation of the audience who listen to the piece, to make pure, white light.

A contemporary of Arvo Part, the composer John Cage (1912–1992) created musical works that expound on ideas of relativity and the philosophical implications that extend beyond science, into the realm of Buddhist philosophy and art.

A singularly inventive and much beloved American composer, John Cage's influence, although already profound, has yet to be fully felt. From around 1950, and throughout the passing years, Cage departed from the pragmatism of precise musical notation and circumscribed ways of performance. His principal contribution to the history of music is his systematic establishment of the principle of indeterminacy. By adapting Zen Buddhist practices to composition and performance, Cage succeeded in bringing both authentic spiritual ideas and a liberating attitude of play to musical enterprise and the wider art world.

In 1992 Cage produced a film, applying his ideas about random musical composition to light. He describes the film, titled *One*[11], comparing its characteristics to those of light: '*One*[11] is a film without subject. There is light but no persons, no things, no ideas about repetition and variation. It is meaningless activity which is nonetheless communicative, like light itself, escaping our attention as communication because it has no content. Light is, as McLuhan said, pure information, without any content to restrict its transforming and informing power.'

One[11] was produced by the German production company Lohner Ranger and premiered on September 19, 1992, in Cologne, with the WDR Orchestra performing Cage's *103*, composed one year earlier and with which it is frequently simultaneously performed.

The film was shot at FSM television studio in Munich by cameraman Van Carlson of Los Angeles, under the direction of Henning Lohner. The film was shown alone at Symphony Space in New York (with a tape of the WDR performance of *103*), on November 1, 1992, and at Cage's memorial *Cagemusicircus*, an event organized by John Kennedy and Essential Music.

In describing the making of the film, Cage said: 'Chance operations were used with respect to the shots, black and white, taken in the FSM television studio in Munich by Van Carlson, a Los Angeles cameraman. The producer and director was Henning Lohner. The executive producer was Peter Lohner. The light environment was designed and programmed by John Cage and Andrew Culver, as was the editing of the film, done in video format at Laser Edit East in New York.'

Stephen Vitiello, a third contemporary composer, has also become known for works which interpret the relationship between music and light. Vitiello is among the most versatile younger artists in the medium of contemporary 'sound work.' Born in New York in 1964, Vitiello started playing in punk and noise bands in the 1970s and later collaborated on projects with the multimedia artist Tony Oursler. In 1991, he organized a concert with the video artist Nam June Paik and the Bad Brains. In the late 1990s, Vitiello began to operate as a solo artist and composer of site-specific work using sound.

Vitiello's piece in the 2002 Whitney Biennial, *World Trade Center Recordings: Winds After Hurrican Floyd,* derives from a 1999 artist residency on the 91st floor of Tower One, where he recorded sounds inside and outside the building. At his 91st-floor studio in Tower One, Vitiello was struck by his view of New York. What he couldn't get over, however, was how flat and unreal the view was. He set about finding some way of 'unflattening the view.' He achieved it by translating light into sound. Vitiello started working with light as a result of his search for a way of interpolating the World Trade Towers.

'It was only when I recognized the silence, shut in by windows that could not be opened, that I found a clue to how I should proceed. The challenge was to bring the sound from outside in, through very thick, sealed windows.'

Vitiello made two sets of recordings of the Towers. The first was achieved by affixing contact microphones to the windows. The second set of recordings was done with a technician and friend, Bob Bielecki. In this second set of recordings Vitiello searched for a way to respond with sound to the lights that he saw after dusk. A small photocell wired to audio cables pointed into the eye of a telescope enabled Vitiello to locate and transform light frequencies into sounds. 'Listening' to the buildings through the medium of light Vitiello found a way to record an intimate experience with a tower that had, initially, been oppressive and distant.

On Vitiello's CD recording, *Bright and Dusty Things,* light becomes sound when passed through a 'light pen.' A photocell is a device that a photographer uses to measure light levels.

For *Bright and Dusty Things* Vitiello pointed a photocell at lights in his studio, including the green and red lights on his mixing board, setting the basis for improvisations. Once the photocell tone was established in the room, Vitiello brought musicians Pauline Oliveros and David Tronzo on board to collaborate with his light beams. Vitiello created the tracks for *Bright and Dusty Things* by asking the musicians to listen carefully to his previously recorded 'light' tracks from the World Trade Tower, and respond with their own 'light improvisations.' Light was the fourth, and most prominent, player in the recording sessions for *Bright and Dusty Things.*

Vitiello continues to develop sound pieces based on his interpretations of light. For his CD, *Light from Falling Cars,* Vitiello recorded the light beams from headlights of cars driving over the Brooklyn Bridge at night.

In 2004 Stephen Vitiello mounted an installation featuring sound generated through light at the Cartier Foundation in Paris. Eight solar cells mounted around the perimeter of a room translated light frequencies into sound, which was then transmitted to a microphone in the street outside the gallery.

Stephen Vitiello, John Cage, and Arvo Part used light as a medium to produce sound. These inventive interpretations of the visual medium of light enable listen-

Above ▪ *View from World Trade Center: Night View,* Stephen Vitiello, courtesy of the artist.

Left ▪ *Solar Cell 1,* Stephen Vitiello, courtesy of the artist.

Light is a key aspect of the drama that is stagecraft. Through the thoughtful use of light an audience can be made to focus on a person or a concept on stage.

ers to 'hear' their environment through a series of inventive, aural images.

THEATER AND LIGHT

Theater takes everyday life and makes it larger. Light is a key aspect of the drama that is stagecraft. Through the thoughtful use of light an audience can be made to focus on a person or a concept on stage. By darkening a stage and creating a single focal point of light a single performer within a crowd becomes a focus.

The word theater is derived from the Greek *theaomai*, 'to see,' and the word spectator is derived from the Latin *spectare*, which means 'to look.' The classic Greek theater was built in the open air, usually on a hillside, and placed so that the afternoon sunlight came from behind the audience and flooded the performing area with light. Until the sixteenth century the theater continued to be basically an outdoor institution.

Borrowing effects from Rembrandt and other painters, theater designers began to 'paint with light'—putting light where it created greater dramatic effect. Today light serves as a unifying medium for the stage. It is a mobile and changing accent that reinforces the action, sustains a mood, and focuses the attention of the audience.[7]

One of the most innovative practitioners in the use of light to create theater is Robert Wilson, who includes light as an important staple in his repertoire of theatrical invention. As Wilson explains: 'Everything begins with light—without light there's no space. And space can't exist without time: they are part of one thing.'[8]

Wilson founded the Watermill Center on Long Island where he works on theatrical productions and hosts conferences, including the Aventis Triangle Forum, for scientists. This meshing of the arts and sciences allows Wilson to pursue innovations in theater through the thoughtful use of light.

In July 1996 a workshop was convened at Wilson's Watermill Center to discuss a means of defining the Cultural District of Pittsburgh, Pennsylvania, using light. Wilson believed that light as a poetic medium would define the space inhabited by visitors to the District. This project was sponsored by Carnegie Mellon University, Carnegie Institute, the City of Pittsburgh, foundations, and corporations.

Collaborating with architect Richard Gluckman, Wilson devised a multi-dimensional, multi-scaled light installation as part of a larger program commissioned by the Pittsburgh Cultural Trust to breathe new life into the city's historic downtown.

For the Pittsburgh project Wilson and Gluckman extended ideas about theatrical lighting beyond the controlled interior of a theater to the street and the city. Light became a means of establishing cohesiveness in a district consisting of many different aesthetics and ideas.

The work was an attempt to establish a new image of the city of Pittsburgh, a former coal-mining town. The Pittsburgh Project is an attempt to give the community a new identity as a 'city of light.'

Prior to the Pittsburgh project, one of Wilson's most famous productions focused on the most influential contemporary theory of light. Albert Einstein's theory of relativity was the focus of Wilson's 1976 production, *Einstein on the Beach.* Premiered in July 1976, in Avignon, France, *Einstein on the Beach* was presented by the Byrd Hoffman Foundation, in association with the Festival d'Avignon, Venice Biennale, and the Region of Lombardy.

Written and directed by Robert Wilson, with music by Phillip Glass, *Einstein on the Beach* presented a new approach to musical theater. The structure of the work has a mathematical precision and dreamlike, allusive content. The play is a precise statement of light, movement, design, and duration.

Einstein's life revolved around the brilliant application of mathematical formulae to natural phenomena. his most important discovery, the theory of relativity, changed life in the twentieth century. Wilson's play, *Einstein on the Beach,* is a mapping of changes wrought by Einstein's investigations and discoveries.

At the core of relativity is light, and the speed of light. Movement throughout the play references the speed of light. Relativity's overarching cultural implications are presented as a continuous march of cultural change and technological advancement as the play proceeds.

Just as light was the central focus of Albert Einstein's work, so it is also a central theme in the work of Wilson—a brilliant, unpredictable, and challenging artist of the theater.

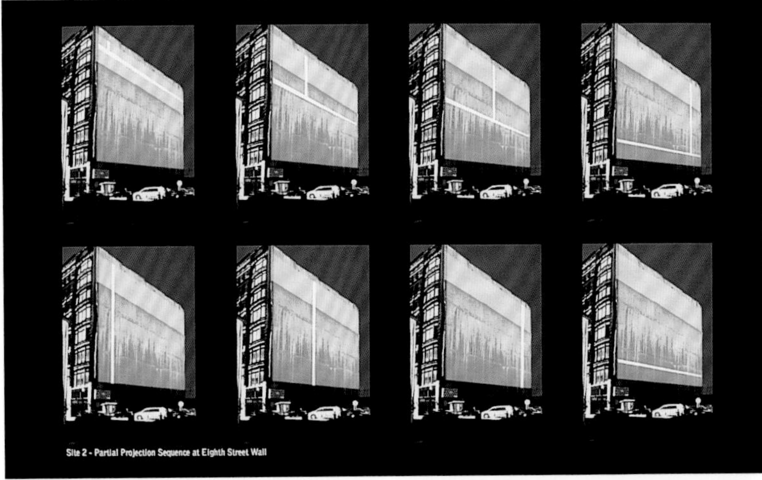

Left ▪ Robert Wilson and Richard Gluckman, sketch view for future light installation in Pittsburgh, from a workshop at Watermill, July 7, 1996. The Pittsburgh Cultural Trust.

Below left and light ▪ Robert Wilson and Richard Gluckman, installation in Pittsburgh Cultural Trust, Pittsburgh, 2001.

Architecture and Light

The history of great architecture is about buildings that adapt creatively to light. One focus of architecture is the connection between what people see and a building's construction. Architects rely on light and its ability to reveal form as a way of creating that connection.

European Gothic churches inspire awe as an architecture of color and light. Gothic architects reduced the mass of their cathedrals to lines of structure in order to maximize the area of glass. Cathedrals were representations of the universe, and the light flooding into them through stained-glass windows held together the Medieval world with light.

During the Renaissance, domes representing the heavens dominated church construction. Light brought in through the oculi and other light sources enhanced the sense that the dome above the nave was a recreated sky, framed and imbued with metaphysical properties. The dome is where the appearance of divine light was expected and symbolized. In addition to capturing divine light, Renaissance churches were also used by contemporary scientists such as Galileo for optical experiments. Several Renaissance church roofs in Italy have holes where light beams enter so that on certain saints' days a line of light traces a path through the church, a tribute to God and to science.

In the eighteenth century the French architect Etienne-Louis Boullée designed a 'Cenotaph to Newton' (1784). This conceptual building, never realized, was a celebration of

Newton's research on light. The building was conceived as a perfect sphere, with apertures representing galaxies in a spherical skin. During the day one could stand inside the sphere and view the stars. At night the sphere sent out beams of light celebrating Newton's accomplishments.

Modern architecture follows this march toward transparency and opening to light and nature through the use of steel framing, the diminishment of mass, and an extensive use of glass. Mies van der Rohe's Farnsworth House—an all-glass house in Plano, Illinois—is probably the most famous example of this modernist ideal.

Glass tends to seem invisible, and architects' fascination with transparency has led to a concentration on invisibility and reduction. The thread that links the history of achievement in architecture is the search for new ways to celebrate the intersection between the wall and nature; to capture the moment and to frame the place where light enters the building.

The following chapters present varying aspects of light in architecture. We begin with Color, and continue with Lines, Form, Glass, Windows, Sky Frames, Shadows and, finally, Reflections. Each chapter presents projects that show how architects have manipulated this life-giving aspect of nature to make its presence palpable as the focus of architecture.

Color

Left ▪ Hanrahan Meyers Architects, Red Hook Center for the Arts, Brooklyn, New York: the intersection between an interior skylight and an exterior window. Colors—yellow and red—appear on the surface of the soffits. The red surface is the result of reflection—the surface itself is painted white. The building establishes a play between surfaces that are colored through reflected and applied colors.

Opposite ▪ Hanrahan Meyers Architects, Red Hook Center for the Arts: the surface of the wall, which appears to be red, registers reflected color from the skylight.

Color and light were explored in Medieval cathedrals, where stained glass windows illustrated Biblical books in bays of the building. Color, a precious commodity during the Middle Ages, created a sense of awe in these buildings, adding to the sense of theater generated by the scale of the space and the structure. Color and light were seen by Medieval church designers as direct representations of the divine spirit. ▪ In contemporary architecture, color and light still inspire awe, in secular settings as well as religious ones. The work of color and light artists such as James Turrell and Dan Flavin has involved the general public in a celebration of light and its physical properties as an exciting formal element of architecture. This enjoyment of light and its constituent colors is a component of several contemporary architectural projects.

Left and opposite ▪ Hanrahan Meyers Architects, Red Hook Center for the Arts: the building entrance is also a gallery. This view looks toward the gallery, which is separated from the entry vestibule by a red, plaster-finished wall.

Left ▪ Hanrahan Meyers Architects, Schrom Television Studios, Queens, New York: the view from the conference room looking toward an interior gallery space. The room appears to be yellow. The color of the room is created by the skylight above, which has a filter that can be controlled electronically to create yellow or white light.

Above ▪ Hanrahan Meyers Architects, Schrom Television Studios: a detailed view looking into the 'light cone,' situated just below the filtered skylight.

Hanrahan Meyers Architects, Schrom Television Studios: from different perspectives in the gallery, looking toward the conference room, with its 'light cone'.

Below left and right ▪ Hanrahan Meyers Architects, Schrom Television Studios: this view looks into the gallery, toward the television stage area. Colors in selected locations throughout the space are reflected and participate in the creation of a spectrum of light.

Left ▪ Steven Holl Architects, Sarphatistraat Offices, Amsterdam: colored lights in the corners of the space, juxtaposed to actual windows, create a play of color and light that question which 'openings' define windows, and which are objects that insinuate spaces beyond. The project is an exploration of 'porous architecture' inscribed with a concept from Morton Feldman's music, 'Patterns in a Chromatic Field.'

Right ▪ Steven Holl Architects, Sarphastistraat Offices: view from one corner of the space, with the entrance below. Rectangular openings, surface mounted lights, and areas of reflected color create a space where the depth of field of the windows and other apertures is questioned. Color animates an otherwise minimalist white room.

Left ▪ Hanrahan Meyers Architects, Schrom Television Studios: the architects designed the east-facing wall of the studio as a 'light wall,' pierced by a series of variously sized apertures, each lined with different colored surfaces. The wall is four feet thick, and the apertures vary in size from six inches square to four feet long by two feet high, with surfaces cut at various angles to the exterior window wall behind.

Below ▪ Hanrahan Meyers Architects, Arts International: this view looks toward the gallery and performance space from the entrance. Red light washes the floor, projected from a window behind the gallery.

Opposite ▪ Hanrahan Meyers Architects, Arts International, New York: walls painted in bright blues and reds adjacent to exterior windows reflect colored light into the gallery, which is, otherwise, a minimalist white room. A blackened, highly polished floor reflects the colored lights.

Lines

Geometry is one of the architect's primary tools for making statements in space. Le Corbusier published manuals on the topic, titled 'The Modulor.' Lines are the most basic elements of geometry. ▪ The following projects make extensive use of lines of light. Combining the basic form with light results in powerful spaces.

Michael Gabellini, Jil Sander Worldwide Showroom, Atelier and Offices in Milan: at the entrance to the space, a line of natural daylight marks the edge between the stair hall and the public space.

John Pawson, Walsh House, Telluride: the fireplace is long and horizontal. The mantel accentuates the horizontality of the composition. This includes the light that is mounted behind the stone, which casts a line of light along the wall. At the top of the wall occupied by the fireplace, Pawson creates a gap that he again accentuates with light.

Michael Gabellini, Jil Sander Showroom: the linearity of the exterior wall is emphasized by the slot of space created by pulling the ceiling back from the exterior wall.

Michael Gabellini, Jil Sander Showroom: another view of the same space, showing the interior surfaces. The room is a composition of horizontal lines, marked using light.

Left ▪ Michael Gabellini, Jil Sander Showroom: the ceiling differentiates the room into different zones using light.

Opposite ▪ Michael Gabellini, Jil Sander Showroom: this view looks toward the public staircase. A line of light at the corner of the room, at the stair landing, defines the vertical circulation.

Opposite ▪ Hiroaki Ohtani, Layer House, Kobe, Japan: a slated skylight allows the sun to cast patterns on the walls.

Right ▪ Hiroaki Ohtani, Layer House, Kobe, Japan.

Opposite and left ▪ Hiroaki Ohtani, Layer House, Kobe, Japan.

Opposite ▪ Kalach and Alvarez architects, 666 House, Mexico: the strong Mexican light in contrast to the heaviness of masonry construction creates opportunities to bring strong lines of light into interior spaces.

Right ▪ Rick Joy, architect, 400 Rubio Avenue, Tucson, Arizona: a line of light enters through the corner of the room, defining the edge between two heavy planes of the exterior shell. This is the architect's studio, which he describes as 'a building of walls, but with blurred boundaries—earthen walls and glass walls, all reaching to the sky… .'

Rick Joy, architect, Pima Canyon House, Tucson, Arizona.

Bohlin Cywinski Jackson,
Bohlin Residence, Waverly,
Pennsylvania.

Form

Below ▪ Joseph Giovannini, Giovannini Loft: a series of sculptural forms define space and serve as functional objects.

Opposite ▪ Joseph Giovannini, Giovannini Loft: dining area.

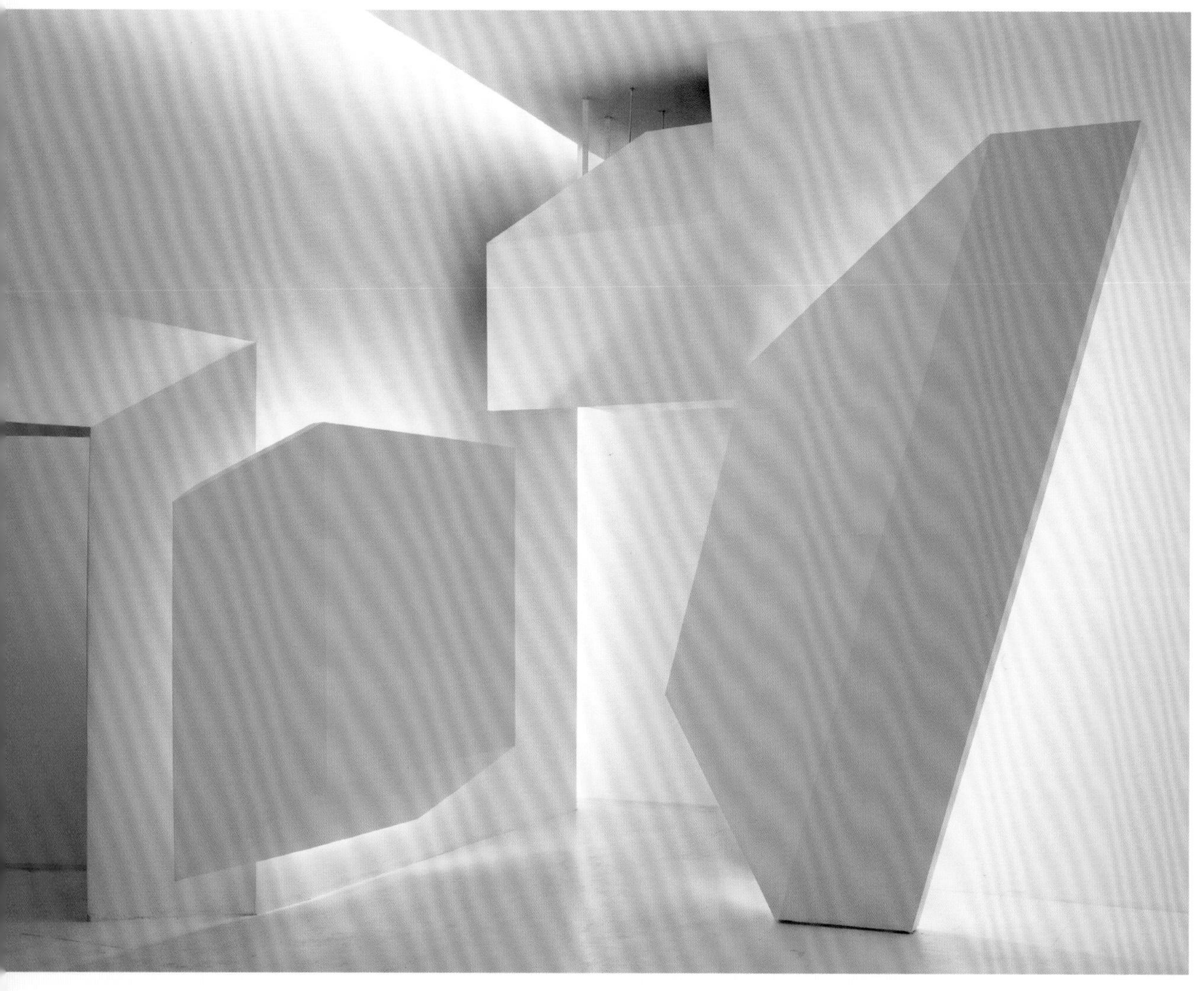

As a painter, sculptor, and architect Michelangelo Buonarotti used light as an integral part of his spatial compositions. At the tomb of Guiliano de' Medici, the Laurentian Library Ricetto, and the dome of St. Peter's in Rome, Michelangelo sculpted space both literally and with light. Gianlorenzo Bernini used light as an important component of sculpture and architecture. In *The Ecstasy of St. Theresa*, the Cornaro Chapel, and the Scala Regia at the Vatican, carved surfaces of sculpture and architecture are manipulated to receive and render light dramatically. The Baroque era made use of light in a manner that echoed to the revelations of contemporary science, including the discoveries of Descartes, Newton, Galileo, Kepler, and Pascal. Through the physical discoveries of this era, the religious significance of light was diminished, but it became instead a metaphor for truth. ▪ In the following pages contemporary works are presented that display a similar aim, with surfaces rendered dramatically by light. These expressionistic projects produce active and restless spatial paradigms that explore light as an element of form-making. A post-modernist attitude toward light, as we move into an era where the speed of light can be fully manipulated, is evident.

Below ▪ Joseph Giovannini, Giovannini Loft: the sculptural form of the main living space creates a dialogue with the owners' collection of minimalist and abstract art.

Right ▪ Joseph Giovannini, Giovannini Loft: looking toward the main sitting room from the living space, light cuts through, marking edges of forms and supplying ambient light.

Joseph Giovannini, Giovannini Loft: the space is as much a play on abstract form as the art in the collection. A skylight brings light into the space as part of the overall abstract composition. Throughout the apartment, light defines the formal composition of the space.

Opposite ▪ Steven Holl Architects, Simmons Hall, MIT, Cambridge, Massachusetts: a stair that moves like a piece of sculpture. A perforated metal baluster accentuates the formal play of the stair, casting light over it and accentuating its undulating form.

This page ▪ Charles Deaton, Deaton House: the very fluid form of this stair crafted out of poured-in-place concrete, registers in light. The blackened handrail helps to delineate the sculptural form.

Opposite ▪ Michael Gabellini, Davide Cenci Boutique, Rome, Italy: the organic shape of the stairs is accentuated by the placement of skylights and clerestory lights above.

Below ▪ Steven Holl Architects, Simmons Hall: a student lounge on an upper floor of the dormitory. Organic forms situate themselves in the gridded massing of the building, and create organically shaped public spaces for use as student lounge areas. The rooms are vessels that channel light into the building's public areas. Light accentuates the organic forms of the plaster surfaces.

Opposite ▪ Steven Holl Architects, Simmons Hall: the undulating main public stair, from below. The poured-in-place concrete form of the stair undulates through the public space. Light pours in through the surrounding abstract, grid wall that simulates the pixelation of a computerized image.

Right ▪ Steven Holl Architects, Simmons Hall: the square apertures that let in the light contrast with the organic form of the stair.

Glass

The artist Marcel Duchamp's sculpture, *The Large Glass*, was prescient in its use of glass as a medium for a work of art that operates simultaneously as a dissertation on future cultural ideals. *The Large Glass* was itself a narrative about relativity, and included in its construction ideas about industrial production (*The Large Glass* was fabricated from a mass-produced, industrial steel-frame glass window). At around the same time that Duchamp's sculpture was presented in the public realm, glass and transparency became the basis for early twentieth century movements in architecture. ▪ Modernism in contemporary architecture is intimately tied to the use of glass. Glass creates the least obtrusive barrier between inside and outside. Its transparency glass allows light to penetrate into interior space while maintaining a visual connection with the outside world. ▪ Contemporary advances in glass technologies include electrostatic glass walls, where a flick of a wall switch can make a glass wall change from transparent to translucent. Invisible electrostatic films applied to the surface of windows can also generate heat across the surface of the glass, so that windows become an interior radiant heat source. ▪ NASA's development of high-strength ceramics for the Space Shuttle Program has resulted in the development of structural glass (e-glass): a transparent material with the strength of steel. Glass floors, swimming -pool enclosures, and other structures are becoming part of the contemporary ouvre. Bearing in mind the need for sustainable structures, e-glass is available in double- and triple-paned units that provide environmentally sound-proof enclosures with the ability to perform as weather-resistant surfaces equal to much heavier materials such as masonry. Modernist architecture continues to move closer to an idealized condition of pure transparency. ▪ Glass, which today seems ubiquitous, was once a rare material used only sparingly in ancient structures. Through advances in industrial production techniques, glass has become readily available as a contemporary building material. Today, a primary mark of a building's modernist sensibilities relates to how glass is used. This section presents examples of several innovative contemporary uses of glass.

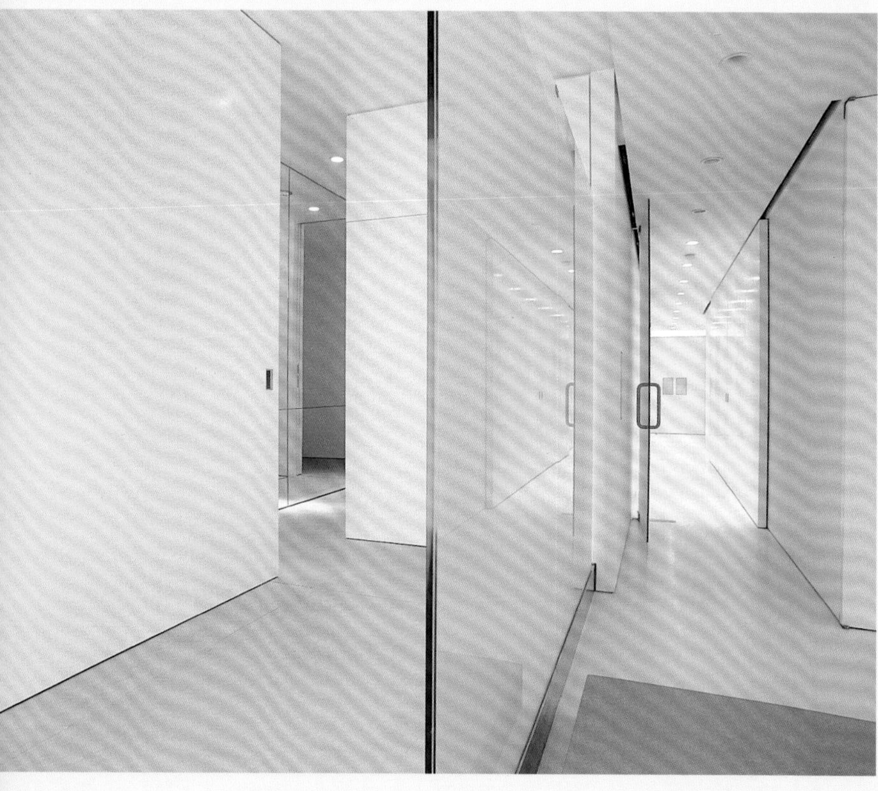

Opposite ▪ Daniel Rowan and Frank Lupo, White Apartment, New York: a wall of etched glass creates privacy, while allowing light and a sense of transparency to divide the space.

Left ▪ Michael Gabellini, Olympic Tower Residence, New York: a plane of etched structural glass separates the kitchen from the dining area. This is set at a 90-degree angle to the exterior curtain wall, with views to the city beyond.

music

Opposite ▪ Bohlin, Cywinski, Jackson, Apple Store, Soho, New York: the transparency of the structural glass stair against the etched structural glass floor creates a composition that is fluid, reflective, and ephemeral.

Right ▪ Bohlin, Cywinski, Jackson, Apple Store, North Michigan Avenue, Chicago: view of the store entrance, from behind the stair. Lit from below, the stair treads suffuse light.

Opposite ▪ Bohlin, Cywinski, Jackson, Forest House, Connecticut.

Right ▪ Hiroyuki Arima + Urban Fourth, Second Plate House, Fukuoka, Japan: a small glazed bridge links the entry foyer to the living room.

Left ▪ Hanrahan Meyers Architects, White Space: this view looks toward the living room from the entry area, which is extended by a structural glass floor. A transluscent glass wall marks the partition between the master bath/bedroom area and living area.

Above ▪ Michael Gabellini, 785 Park Avenue Residence, New York.

Right ▪ Hanrahan Meyers Architects, White Space: detail view of the translucent glass wall in the master bath.

Far right ▪ Hanrahan Meyers Architects, White Space: a detail view of the glass wall separating the kitchen from the dining area.

Below ▪ Hanrahan Meyers Architects, DelMonico/ Washburn Residence, New York: a glass wall separates the master bedroom from the public living space. The open area of the bedroom joins a south-facing window. A sense of continuous glass and light marks the end of the living space.

Opposite ▪ Hanrahan Meyers Architects, Arts International Headquarters: the glass wall at the end of the conference room is almost invisible. The adjacent wall is also able to 'disappear' by being movable. When the arts organization needs to expand the adjacent public space, the conference room can be packed up, like a suitcase, and disappear.

Hanrahan Meyers Architects, Schrom Studios, New York: this is the end elevation of the conference room, looking toward the east 'light wall.'

Left ▪ Hanrahan Meyers Architects, Holley Residence, New York: a glass wall separates the master bedroom and master bath.

Right ▪ Hanrahan Meyers Architects, Holley Residence: the glass wall separates the master bedroom from the public space. In the public space the only full-height wall is the glass wall.

Opposite ▪ Rick Joy, 400 Rubio Avenue, Tucson, Arizona: a glass wall separates an exterior courtyard space from an interior space. The two spaces appear to flow together into one.

Right ▪ Hiroyuki Arima + Urban Fourth, Second Plate House and studio, Fukuoka, Japan. Thin ceiling and wall planes appear to pull apart.

Opposite ▪ Hanrahan Meyers Architects, White Space: a composition of different types of glass, including handmade glass tiles, a free-standing glass plane, and a frameless sheet of translucent glass in the master bath.

Left ▪ Hanrahan Meyers Architects, White Space: hand-made cast-glass tiles frame a view toward Central Park.

Below ▪ Hanrahan Meyers Architects, White Space: a detail view of the structural glass floor.

Right ▪ Hanrahan Meyers Architects, White Space: a view toward the entry with structural glass floor in the foreground.

Windows

Windows mark the most prominent difference between classical and contemporary architecture. Prior to the twentieth century most buildings were constructed using bearing walls, greatly restricting the size and the placement of glass and windows. Twentieth-century steel construction techniques allowed windows to be a much freer element in the façade of buildings, and the expression of joining the interior to the exterior space became a paradigm for modernism. Le Corbusier, one of the most famous architects of the modernist movement in twentieth-century architecture, felt this freedom so strongly that he made the reinterpretation and reinvention of modern windows a strategic part of his architecture. ▪ The window was also portrayed as an icon of modernism in Marcel Duchamp's *The Large Glass*. By addressing the theory of relativity and the philosophical changes inferred by contemporary physics, *The Large Glass* set the window as the arena of philosophical discourse for architects whose work followed. ▪ The pages that follow present images of contemporary windows that address the constructional implications of contemporary technologies. How architects detail and insert the language of the window into their designs frames their position to contemporary theories and dialogues about the meaning of space in the contemporary world.

Left ▪ Michael Gabellini, Architect, Jill Sander Worldwide Showroom, Atelier and Offices in Milan: a glowing white light makes an abstract composition with the window that sits adjacent to the stair. The window becomes a minimalist object, a simple square punch in the wall.

Opposite ▪ TEN Arquitectos, Hotel Habita, Mexico City, Mexico: a window with an etched finish creates a screen, allowing suffused light to enter through the etched portions of the glass. In an urban setting, where privacy is an issue, the etched surface of the glass creates privacy while the clear portion allows a partial view.

Opposite ▪ Hanrahan Meyers Architects, White Space: a bedroom window overlooking Central Park, New York.

Right ▪ Michael Gabellini. Olympic Tower Residence, New York.

Marcio Kogan, BR House, Araras, Brazil: a large plate-glass window gives a view toward Atlantic Rain Forest.

Below left and right ▪ Simon Conder Associates, London, Nicholson Garden Room: the project is the garden of an existing house in north London. The Garden Room is a simple glass box that feels part of the garden it sits within.

Rick Joy, Catalina House, Tucson, Arizona: the thickness of the tamped earth construction is apparent wherever windows interrupt the solid walls. A square frame gives a view to the landscape around the house.

Marcio Kogan, BR House,
Araras, Brazil.

Opposite ▪ IL Kim, *The White Box*: a window view from the living room toward the courtyard..

Below ▪ IL Kim, Tokyo House: the study window.

Above ▪ John Pawson, Walsh House, Telluride, Colorado: the windows mark the perimeter of the room. The architect uses common windows in a strong, minimalist and simple way.

Opposite ▪ Adria, Broid, Rojkind, F-2 House: a minimalist and sculptural room, framed in concrete. Frameless glass fills the openings in the concrete wall, creating views to nature.

Above ▪ Hanrahan Meyers Architects, Holley House: the wall in the foreground marks the edge of a pavilion that creates the entry to the house to the north, and houses guest bedrooms. The large opening to the yard looks into the guest bedroom hallway.

Left ▪ Hanrahan Meyers Architects, Holley House: view of the window to the living area. 12-foot (3.6-metre) high walls of glass and cypress enclose two pavilions that house the main living spaces of the house.

Hanrahan Meyers Architects, Holley House: a view toward the living area. A 12-foot (3.6-metre) high wall of sliding glass panels looks out toward nature. An aperture through the living room's stone fireplace creates a space for storing wood, and gives a view toward the nature beyond.

Sky Frames

In Renaissance, Baroque, and Rococo architecture the dome, its oculi, and the lantern above were the focus of attention. Bringing the sky down into the building interior, creating a frame for it, and making a story from how the heavens are presented through a painted cycle on the face of the dome, was a central focus for these buildings. ■ In contemporary architecture light is also brought in from above, but in a more objective, naturalistic way. The early modernist Alvar Aalto was particularly skilled in bringing light from skylights into his buildings in a way that celebrated light as a piece of 'found' nature. The projects that follow are successful in bringing the sky and, by extension, nature into dialogue with contemporary spaces.

Andrew Berman, architect, Whitespace Studios, New York: a brutalist minimalist space, where cuts in the ceiling provide the main sense of connection between inside and outside. The space is a former stables and the architect has added a second and third floor, including extensive skylights.

Andrew Berman, architect, Whitespace Studios: the line of the skylights picks up the line of the window.

IL Kim, architect, *The White Box*: a view showing a 'sky frame.'

Left ▪ Steven Holl Architects, Sarphatistraat Offices in Amsterdam: the skylights accentuate the space as a random composition of color and light.

Above ▪ Steven Holl Architects, Sarphatistraat Offices in Amsterdam: looking up at the ceiling, the skylights are covered in a film of perforated metal. The perforated metal becomes a unifying skin covering and uniting all surfaces.

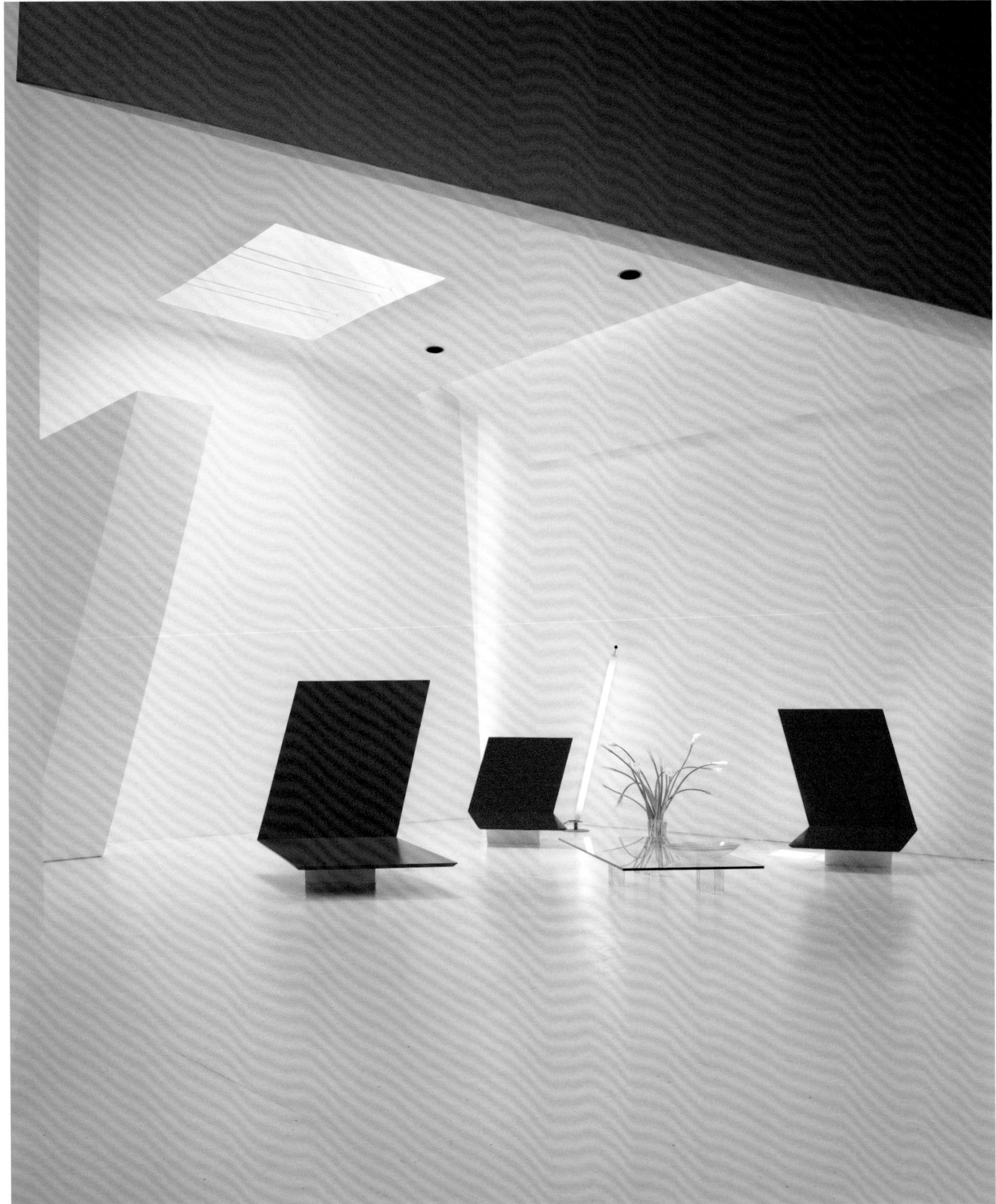

Left ▪ Joseph Giovannini, Giovannini Loft: the skylight above becomes another form, animating the space.

Opposite ▪ Raphael Moneo, Cathedral of Our Lady of the Angels, Los Angeles: a window folds up into the ceiling and becomes a skylight.

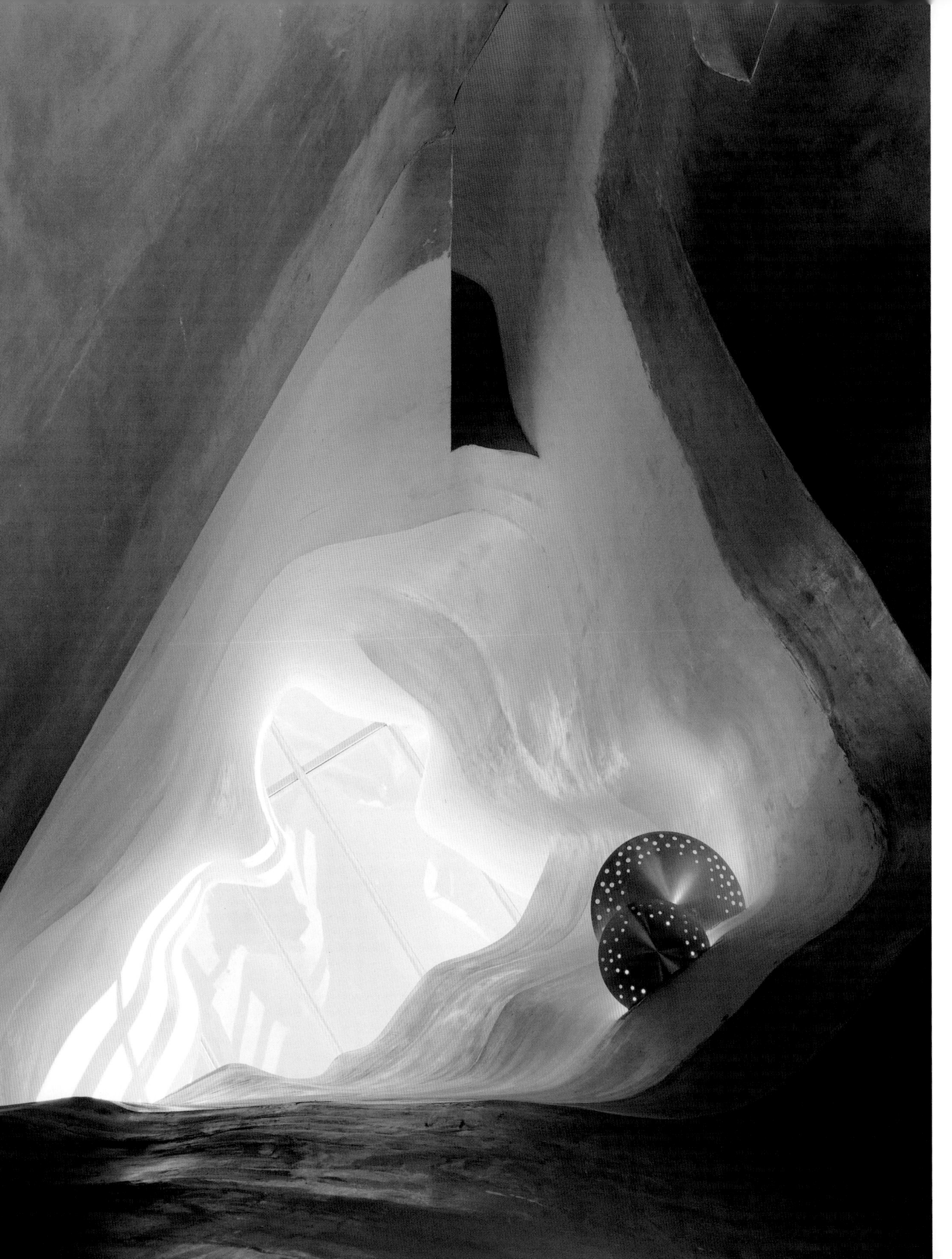

Steven Holl Architects, Simmons Hall, MIT, Cambridge, Massachusetts: an organically shaped opening onto the sky is created. Light washes down over an organic three-dimensional form below.

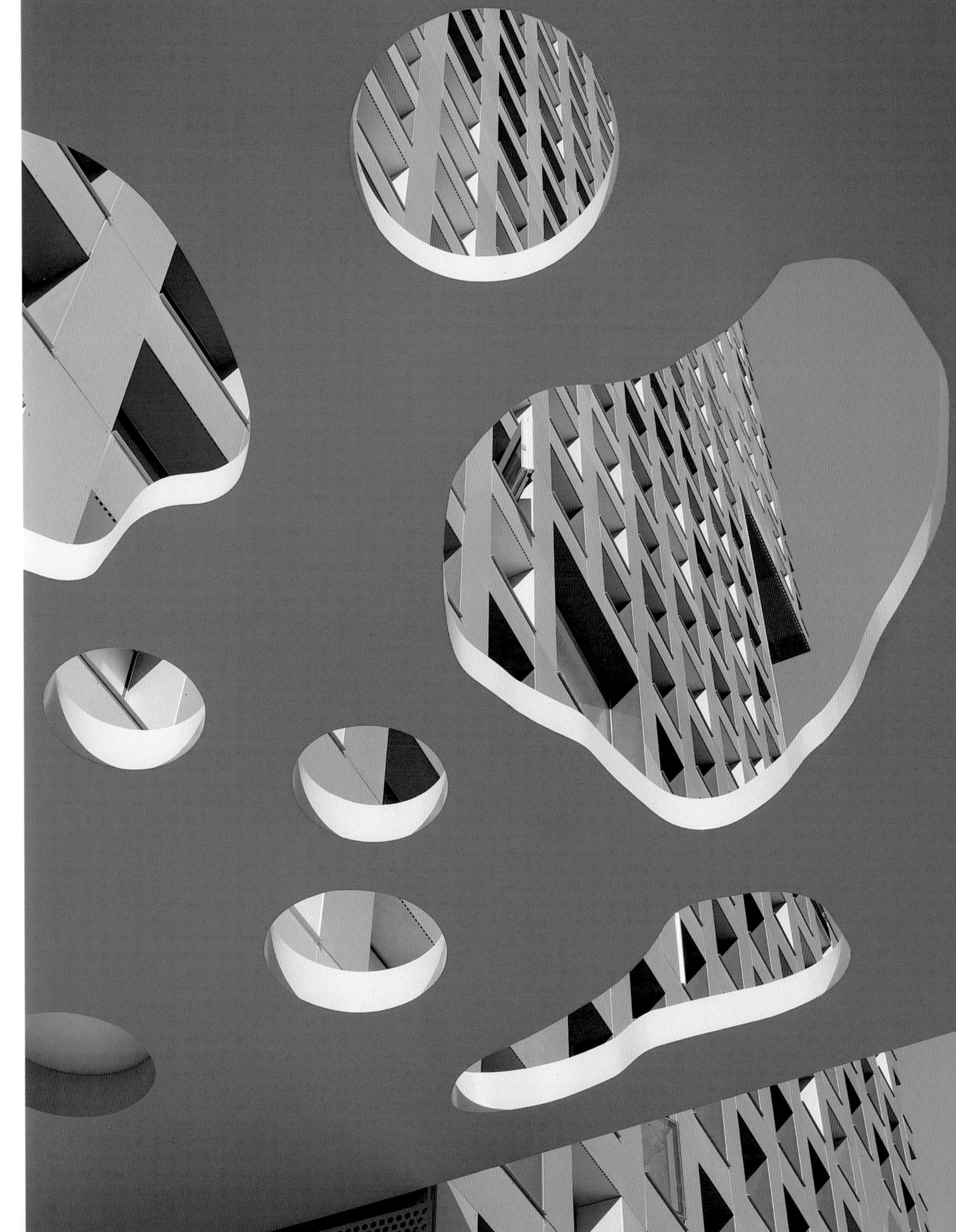

Steven Holl Architects, Simmons Hall: organic, random openings in the building canopy make reference to the organic forms inside the building.

Shadows

Below ▪ Ricardo Legorreta, Greenberg House: a row of columns at the edge of an aperture generate strong linear shadows.

Opposite ▪ Ricardo Legorreta, Greenberg House: another view of the collonade shows how the bright light of the southwest United States makes shadows that cut sharp figures. Shadows become important formal elements in the space, equal in value to solid walls and columns.

Shadows create drama and emphasize light. At the Shrine of the Sybil in Delphi, Greece, a series of tall arches carved into the face of a mountain made dramatic lines of shadow and light. When the Sybil appeared she stood at the end of this row of arches, shadows emphasizing the length of the hall of the Shrine, and screamed answers to questions posed by sycophants. The hypostyle halls of Egyptian temples created dramatically shadowed sequences to inner sanctuaries. In Mexico, the Pyramid of Chichen-Itza uses shadow as a means of conveying information. On March 21, the spring solstice, the body of the serpent metaphorically descends from the temple on top of the pyramid and arrives at the heads at the foot of the staircase. ▪ Shadows are transitory, moving forms that depend on a source of light for their stability. As the sun makes its daily transit from east to west, shadows convey a sense of time. The landscape is constantly changing in response to the seasons, the weather and the time of day. The recording of this movement and change through the reading of form in light, as well as a contemporary unfolding of the phenomena of the physics of sunlight, is presented in the pages that follow.

Left ▪ Rick Joy, Pima Canyon House, Pima Canyon, Arizona: strong southwestern light passing through a linear trellis creates a space striped with bands of light. The interaction between form and light becomes the subject.

Left ▪ E. Fay Jones. Thorncrown Chapel, Eureka Springs, Arkansas: Thorncrown Chapel is nestled in a wooded setting and rises 48 feet high (14.5 metres), with over 6,000 square feet (1,829 square metres) of glass.

Winery, Yountville, California: the winery wall is made from local field stones embedded in a wire wall. Light filtering through the stones creates strong forms on the walls, floor and roof. A view toward the wall gives a sense of the light entering through the gaps between the stones.

Above ▪ Moshe Safdie, National Gallery of Canada, Ottawa, Ontario, Canada: a skylight casts shadows whose dramatic effect is equal to sculpture in the courtyard.

Right ▪ Moshe Safdie, National Gallery of Canada: a skylight with dramatic forms casts shadows, marking an otherwise blank floor with patterns of light.

Below ▪ E. Fay Jones, Thorncrown Chapel: a wood structure opens to allow light to penetrate. The patterning on the ground creates a sense of seamless connection to the surrounding trees.

Opposite ▪ Antoine Predock, Arizona State University, Nelson Fine Arts Museum, Tempe, Arizona: a poured concrete skylight with patterned openings creates a pattern of light in the entrance area for the Nelson Fine Arts Museum. The shadow from the surrounding light screen on the walls, and above, creates patterns that allow sun and air to penetrate the entrance court, while modulating the heat.

Ricardo Legorreta, Architect, Greenberg House: a wood trellis above an outdoor stair creates linear patterning that underlines the rhythm of the treads below.

Following pages: Ricardo Legorreta, Greenberg House: the wood trellis at the edge of an outdoor space creates a frame to a garden.

Reflection

At the Acropolis in Greece, an important part of the architectural sequence from the town below, was through the Propylaea gate, past the Erechthion. The Erechthion contained a pool of water said to have been produced by Poseiden's trident. A pool forms part of a reinterpretation of the Acropolis in Mies van der Rohe's Barcelona Pavilion, where reflection and refraction an important aspect of the architectural composition. The Ames Gatehouse Lodge by H.H. Richardson uses water as part of an overall compositional ode to the importance of the four elements: earth, air, fire and water. Frank Lloyd Wright also references these four elements at Fallingwater and in his design of the Hollyhock House in Los Angeles, California. ▪ In the projects that follow light refracted and/or reflected through water, or other media such as glass, establishes a special mood in the architecture. Refraction generates reflections of light that are bent, fractured and dispersed, lending a special quality to light that allows the viewer to know that water is nearby.

This page ▪ Steven Holl Architects, Sarphatistraat Offices, Amsterdam: the elevation of the Sarphatistraat Offices reflected in the adjacent canal generates a second façade for the building.

Opposite ▪ Steven Holl Architects, Sarphatistraat Offices: colors are magnified in this image that shows the refracted image of the façade. That part of the elevation that is solid disappears and the ephemeral light of the building takes precedence.

Opposite ▪ Steven Holl Architects, Simmons Hall, MIT, Cambridge, Massachusetts: a highly reflective floor reflects points of light from the ceiling.

Above ▪ Hanrahan Meyers Architects, Arts International, New York: the floor is highly polished and blackened so that surfaces reflect in it. Lights on the floor reflect the lights and colors on the walls.

ıa + Urban Fourth,
e House, Fukuoka,
v toward the entry
-inch (5-centimetre)
ng pool in the

Opposite ▪ Hiroyuki Arima + Urban Fourth, Second Plate House, Fukuoka, Japan: the house and studio buildings flank a 2-inch- (5-centimetre) deep, triangular reflecting pool.

Above ▪ Hiroyuki Arima + Urban Fourth, Second Plate House, Fukuoka, Japan: a view toward the reflecting pool from the living room.

Opposite ▪ Marcio Kogan. BR House, Araras, Brazil: a lap pool is sited under the house's main volume.

Above ▪ Marcio Kogan, BR House, Araras, Brazil: the lap pool.

Below ▪ Hanrahan Meyers Architects, Singer Residence Poolhouse, East Hampton, New York: a blue pool of water in front of the poolhouse addition reflects the color of the sky onto the pavilion. The poolhouse itself has a blue wall that mirrors the color of the pool, linking the water to the house.

Opposite ▪ Ricardo Legorreta, Laviada House: a window onto an adjacent garden frames a view of nature. The green from this view is reflected in the foreground pool.

Opposite ▪ Patkau Architects, Vancouver House, Vancouver, British Columbia: a glass-bottomed pool creates a space of reflection.

Right ▪ Patkau Architects, Vancouver House: the glass-bottomed pool is also a skylight to the room below.

Bohlin, Cywinski, Jackson, Mountain Retreat, Park City, Utah: a pool pavilion with a reflective ceiling generates an image of the adjacent natural setting both in the pool and on the pool ceiling.

Opposite ▪ Adria, Broid, Rojkind, F-2 House: the pool's surface merges with the interior space.

Right ▪ IL Kim, *The White Box*: there is a glass walkway to house entry areas.

Opposite ▪ Rick Joy, Tubac House, Tubac, Arizona: a reflecting pool edged in steel makes a similar image to the adjacent exterior window. Both reflect the natural setting.

Right ▪ Rem Koolhaas, Guggenheim Museum, Las Vegas, Nevada: a glass window gives a view to the outdoors. Light is reflected, both in the window and the structural glass floor.

Below ▪ Rick Joy, Catalina House, Tucson, Arizona: soft light filters into the living area accentuating, a modeled wall of tamped earth. The surface modulates softly in the bright desert light which accentuates the wall's square cut-outs.

Right ▪ Rick Joy, Catalina House: an exterior wall with a skylight, looking toward the dining area. A window at the base of the wall accentuates the depth of the tamped earth wall. Light from an overhead skylight washes across the tamped earth surface, accentuating the nature of the material.

Notes and further reading

Notes

1. Forster, Kurt W.: "Light in Architecture" in *Light in Architecture and Art,* Marfa, Texas: The Chinati Foundation, 2002, p. 10

2. Viola, Bill: "*Chott el-Djerid (A Portrait in Light and Heat*" in *Bill Viola* (exhibition catalogue), New York: Whitney Museum of American Art, 1997

3. ibid., p. 120

4. Ragheb, J. Fiona: "Of Situations and Sites" in *The Architecture of Light*, New York: Guggenheim Museum Publications, 1999, p. 14

5. Evans, Robin: *The Projective Cast,* Cambridge: MIT Press, 1995, p. 241

6. Zajonc, Arthur: *Catching the Light: The Entwined History of Light and Mind,* Oxford: Oxford University Press, 1995

7. *Oxford English Dictionary*: see explanatory sections 1–8 on theatre, pp 881–2

8. Lang Ho: "Robert Wilson Sees the Light" in *Architecture*, February, 2000, p. 57

Selected publications, exhibitions and events

John Cage

Writings Through John Cage's Music, Poetry and Art, David W. Bernstein and Christopher Hatch, eds, Chicago: The Universtiy of Chicago Press, 2001

Musicage: John Cage in Conversation with Joan Retallack, Hanover: University Press of New England, 1996

John Cage: Composed in America, Marjo Perloff and Charles Junkerman, eds, Chicago: University of Chicago Press, 1994

The Roaring Silence—John Cage: A Life, David Revill, New York: Arcade Publishing, 1993

John Cage: An Anthology, Richard Kostelanetz, ed., New York: Da Capo Press, 1991

Empty Words: Writings '73–78, John Cage, Middletown: Wesleyan University Press, 1981

Experimental Music: Cage and Beyond, Michael Nyman, New York: Schirmer Books, 1974

Silence: Lectures and Writings, John Cage, Middletown: Wesleyan University Press, 1967

Dan Flavin

Dan Flavin, Michael Govan, London: Serpentine Gallery, 2001

Dan Flavin: The Architecture of Light, J. Fiona Ragheb, ed., New York: Solomon R. Guggenheim Foundation, 1999

Dan Flavin, Dan Flavin, Michael Govan, and Julio Sanchez, Buenos Aires: Fundación Proa, 1998

Dan Flavin: Fluorescent Light, etc., Mel Bochner, Dan Flavin, Donald Judd, and Brydon Smith, Ottawa: National Gallery of Canada for the Queen's Printer, 1969

"Writings by Martial Raysse, Dan Flavin, Robert Smithson" in *Minimal Art: A Critical Anthology*, Gregory Battcock, ed., New York: E.P. Dutton, 1968

Lene Vestergaard Hau

"Frozen Light" in *Scientific American*, Lene Vestergaard Hau, July 2001

"Observation of coherent optical information storage in an atomic medium using halted light pulses" in *Nature*, 409, Hien Liu, Zachary Dutton, Cyrus H. Behroozi, and Lene Vestergaard Hau, 2001

"She Puts the Brakes on Light" in *The New York Times*, Malcom W. Browne, March 30, 1999

"Light speed reduction to 17 metres per second in an ultracold atomic gas", *Nature*, 397, Lene Vestergaard Hau, S.E. Harris, Zachary Dutton, and Cyrus H. Behroozi, 1999

Hanrahan Meyers Architects

Architects design music, presentation of "light score" at the Kitchen Experimental Performance Space, New York, 2004

Pratt Pavilion, AIANY Chapter Design Award, 2004

Wonder Women WaterFall Table, presented at ICFF weekend in New York, 2004

AIANY Chapter, exhibition of Arts International and Schrom Studios, 2002

Four States of Architecture, London: Wiley-Academy, 2002; monograph on Hanrahan Meyers Architects

The Architect, Maggie Toy, Mulgrave: Images Publishing, 2001; featuring V. Meyers' biography and selected projects: Sagaponac, Red Hook Center for the Arts, WaveLine, and MoMA Tower Apartment

Architectural Record, March, 2001; featuring Red Hook Center for the Arts,

Architectural Record, September, 2001; featuring Record Interiors, Schrom Television Studios

Manhattan Lofts, Ivan Richards, London: Wiley-Academy, 2000; featuring Holley Loft (on cover) and MoMA Tower Apartment

"Space and the Perception of Time" in *Journal of Architectural Education*, V. Meyers, November, 1999

The Un-Private House, The Museum of Modern Art: New York, June 1999; exhibition catalog of new housing prototypes and residential design

Architecture for the Next Millennium, exhibition and symposium, American Academy, Rome, 1999

Glasgow 1999, Glasgow, April 1999; invited to participate in publication and exhibition

Lofts: Living and Working Spaces, Francisco Asensio Cerver, Barcelona: Arco Editorial; featuring Holley Loft, 1998

The New American Apartment, New York: Watson-Guptill, 1997; featuring Holley Loft

Designing with Glass, Carol King, ed., New York: Rizzoli, 1996; featuring Holley Loft

581 Architects in the World, Aaron Betsky, coordinator, Tokyo: TOTO Shuppan, 1995; featuring profile of Hanrahan Meyers

Progressive Architecture, Awards Issue, 1993; featuring Inside-Out House and Hudson River House

Emerging Voices in Architecture, Gallery of Functional Art, Santa Monica, California, 1990

Progressive Architecture, Young Architects Issue, 1990; featuring Crafts Production Center

An Interpretive Center, Columbia University, 1989 GSAPP miniseries and exhibition; catalog, J. Ockman, ed.

Light and Heat, group exhibition of artist- and architect-designed lighting fixtures, Gallery 91, New York, 1989

House for Artists, Architectural League, exhibition of work, New York, 1986

Rei Naito
MOT Annual 1999: Modest Radicalism, exhibition catalog, Tokyo: Museum of Contemporary Art, 1999

Rei Naito: One Place on the Earth, exhibition catalog, XLVII Venice Biennale, 1997

Rei Naito: Being Called, Frankfurt am Main: Sonderausstellung des Museums für Moderne Kunst, 1997

"Rei Naito at D'Amelio Terras" in *Art in America*, May 1997

"Impossibility of Art and 'Potential Aspects of Life'" in *Art Today*, 1994

A Quality of Noticing: Rei Naito, Caoimhin Mac Giolla Leith, Llandudno: Oriel Mostyn, 1993

Arvo Part
Ex Oriente: Ten Composers from the Former USSR, Valeria Tsenova, ed., Berlin: E. Kuhn, 2002

Arvo Part (Oxford Studies of Composers), Oxford: Oxford University Press, 1997

"Discovering the Music of Estonian Composer Arvo Part" in *Choral Journal*, August 1993

Contemporary Composers, Brian Morton and Pamela Collins, eds., Chicago: St. James, 1992

Bill Viola
Bill Viola, exhibition catalogue with contributions by Lewis Hyde, Kira Perov, David A. Ross, and Bill Viola, New York: Whitney Museum of American Art, 1997

Reasons for Knocking at an Empty House: Writings, Robert Violette, Bill Viola, eds, Cambridge: MIT Press, 1995

Bill Viola: The Sleep of Reason, exhibition catalog, Jouy-en-Josas: Fondation Cartier pour l'Art Contemporain, 1990

Bill Viola: Statements by the Artist, exhibition catalog, introduction by Julia Brown, Los Angeles: Museum of Contemporary Art, 1985

Bill Viola, exhibition catalog with interview by Deirdre Boyle, Paris: Musée d'Art Moderne de la Ville de Paris, 1983

Bill Viola: Installations and Videotapes, exhibition catalog, Barbara London, ed., New York: Museum of Modern Art, 1987

Stephen Vitiello
"Stephen Vitiello" in *Frieze*, James Trainor, May 2002

"Music Boxes and Photocells in a Land Beyond Time" in *The Village Voice*, Kyle Gann, May 1–7 2002

"Spiritual America, From Ecstatic to Transcendent" in *The New York Times*, Holland Cotter, March 8, 2002

"Music from the 91st Floor" from the article "The View from Downtown" in *The Wire*, Stephen Vitiello, November 2001

Stephen Vitiello, Paulo Herkenhoff, New York: Clocktower Gallery, P.S. 1 Contemporary Art Center, 2001

"Don't Quit Your Day Job", in *New Music Box*, Kenneth Goldsmith, The American Music Center, April 2000

Interview with Tony Oursler, Stephen Vitiello, and Constance De Jong by Lynne Cook, in *Tony Oursler*, Kunstverein Hannover, 1999

Robert Wilson
Robert Wilson, Franco Quadri, Franco Bertoni, Robert Stearns, eds, New York: Rizzoli,1998

"Hamlet as Autobiography, Spoken in Reflective Voice", interview by Marion Kessel in *The New York Times*, July 2, 1995

"Works on Paper" in *Performing Arts Journal*, no.43, vol.15:1, 1993

"A Propos de Doctor Faustus Lights the Lights", excerpt from an in interview in *Theatre/Public*, April 1992

"Robert Wilson: Director, Designer, Theater and Visual Artist, New York City" from an interview by Dodie Kazanjian in *Artsreview: America's Opera*, no5:1, 1988

Text-Sound Texts, Robert Wilson, Richard Kostelanetz eds, New York, 1980

'A Letter for Queen Victoria' in *The Theater of Images*, Bonnie Maranca, ed., New York, 1977

Credits Index

Acknowledgements
I would like to acknowledge and thank Bernard Tschumi, Dean of Columbia's Graduate School of Architecture, Planning and Preservation, as well as David Hinckle, Assistant Dean, for their unwavering support of me and of this project. Without it this book would not have been possible. This project received funding from Columbia's GSAPP.

I would also like to thank Clay Odum, Dan Cheong, Kathy Chang, and Akira Nakamura.

I have had help from various people in the arts community. Special thanks to Betty Freeman, who put me in touch with Arvo Part.

Special thanks as well to James Trulove who acted as the Production Advisor for this book, and to Andy and James at Wayne William Creative who laid out the book. Finally, many thanks to Philip Cooper at Laurence King Publishing.

Picture Credits
Pictures courtesy the artists/architects unless otherwise indicated

2 Schrom Studios, New York
Photo: Peter Aaron/Esto Photographics

7 Chapel of St. Ignatius, Seattle, WA
Photo: Paul Warchol

8 *Reflection*, Mary Temple

9 Prism photograph: Andrew Davidhazy

10 *Chott el-Djerid (A Portrait in Light and Heat)*
Photos: Kira Perov

11 *The Veiling* (sketch)
Sketches: Bill Viola
Photos: Roman Mensing

12 Marfa Project
Photos: Florian Holzherr

13t *One Place on the Earth*, Rei Naito

13b *Reflection*, Mary Temple

14 experiment with light manipulation, Dr. Lene Hau

15t Portrait of Alvo Part
Photo: Harri Rospu

15b Music score, Alvo Part

16 *One*, Lohner Ranger

17t *View from World Trade Center*, Stephen Vitiello

17b *Solar Cell 1*, Stephen Vitiello

19t View for Future Light Installation, Pittsburgh, Robert Wllson and Richard Gluckman

19b Light Installation, Pittsburgh, Robert Wilson and Richard Gluckman

22–25 Red Hook Center for the Arts, New York
Photos: Eduard Hueber

26–29 Schrom Studios, New York
Photos: Peter Aaron/Esto Photographics

30–31 Sarphatistraat Office, Amsterdam
Photos: Paul Warchol

32 Arts International, New York
Photo: Peter Aaron/Esto Photographics

33t Schrom Studio, New York
Photo: Peter Aaron/Esto Photographics

33b Arts International, New York
Photo: Peter Aaron/Esto Photographics

34, 36–39 Jil Sander Worldwide Showroom, Atelier, and Office, Milan, Italy
Lighting designer: Michael Gabellini
Photo: Paul Warchol

35 Walsh House, Telluride, CO
Photo: Undine Prohl

40–43 Layer House, Kobe, Japan
Photo: Kouji Okamoto

44 666 House
Photo: Undine Prohl

45 400 Rubio Avenue,Tucson, AZ
Photo: Bill Timmerman

46 Pima Canyon House, Tucson, AZ
Photo: Bill Timmerman

47 Bohlin Residence, PA
Photo: Mike Thomas

48–53 Giovannini Loft
Photos: Michael Moran

54 Simmons Hall, MIT, Cambridge, MA
Photo: Paul Warchol

55 Deaton House
Photo: Undine Prohl

56 Davide Cenci Boutique, Rome, Italy
Lighting designer: Ross Muir
Photo: Ross Muir

57–59 Simmons Hall, MIT, Cambridge, MA
Photos: Paul Warchol

60 White Apartment
Photo: Michael Moran

61 Olympic Tower Residence, New York
Photo: Paul Warchol

62–63 Apple Store, New York
Photo: Peter Aaron/Esto Photographics

64 Forest House, CT
Photo: Peter Aaron/Esto Photographics

65 Second Plate House, Fukuoka, Japan
Photo: Kouji Okamoto

66, 68–9 White Space, New York
Photo: Michael Moran

67 785 Park Avenue Residence, New York
Photo: Paul Warchol

70 Del Monico (Washburn Residence), New York
Photo: Jordi Miralles

71 Arts International, New York
Photo: Peter Aaron/Esto Photographics

72 Schrom Studio, New York
Peter Aaron/Esto Photographics

73 Holley Loft, New York
Photos: Peter Aaron/Esto Photographics

74 400 Rubio Avenue, Tucson, AZ
Photo: James McGoon

75 Second Plate House, Fukuoka, Japan
Photo: Kouji Okamoto

76–79 White Space, New York
Photos: Michael Moran

80 Jil Sander World Wide Showroom, Atelier, and Office, Milan, Italy
Photo: Paul Warchol

81 Hotel Habita, Mexico City
Photo: Undine Prohl

82 White Space, New York
Photo: Michael Moran

83 Jil Sander World Wide Showroom, Atelier, and Office, Milan, Italy
Photo: Paul Warchol

84 BR House, Araras, Rio de Janeiro, Brazil
Photo: Nelson Kon
Lighting designer: Maneco Quinderé & Ass.

85 Nicholson Garden Room, London, UK
Photo: Chris Gascoigne/VIEW

86 Catalina House, Tucson, AZ
Photo: Bill Timmerman

87 BR House, Araras, Rio de Janeiro, Brazil
Photo: Nelson Kon
Lighting designer: Maneco Quinderé & Ass.

88–89 *The White Box*, Tokyo, Japan
Photos: Toshihiro Komatsu

90 Walsh House, Telluride, CO
Photo: Undine Prohl

91 F-2 House, Mexico City
Photo: Undine Prohl

92–93 Holley House, Garrison, NY
Photos: Michael Moran

94–96 White Space Studios, New York
Photos: Michael Moran

97 *The White Box*, Tokyo, Japan,2004
Photos: Toshihiro Komatsu

98–99 Sarphatistraat Office, Amsterdam
Photos: Paul Warchol

100 Giovannini Loft
Photo: Michael Moran

101 Cathedral of Our Lady, Los Angeles
Photo: Undine Prohl

102–103 Simmons Hall, Cambridge, MA
Photos: Michael Moran

104–105 Greenberg House, Los Angeles
Photos: Timothy Hursley

106 Pima Canyon House, Tucson, AZ
Photo: Bill Timmerman

107 Thorncrown Chapel, Eureka Springs, AR
Photo: Timothy Hursley

108–109 Dominus Winery, Yountville, CA
Photos: Timothy Hursley

110–111 National Gallery of Canada, Ottawa, Ontario
Photo: Timothy Hursley

112 Arizona State University, Neilson Fine Arts Museum, Tempe, AZ
Photo: Timothy Hursley

113 Thorncrown Chapel, Eureka Springs, AR
Photo: Timothy Hursley

114–116 Greenberg House, Los Angeles
Photos: Timothy Hursley

118–119 Sarphatistraat Office, Amsterdam
Photos: Paul Warchol

120 Simmons Hall, Cambridge, MIT, MA
Photo: Paul Warchol

121 Arts International, New York
Photo: Peter Aaron/Esto Photographics

122–125 Second Plate House, Fukuoka, Japan
Photos: Kouji Okamoto

126–127 BR House, Araras, Rio de Janeiro, Brazil
Photos: Nelson Kon
Lighting designer: Maneco Quinderé & Ass.

128 Singer Residence, New York
Photo: Peter Aaron/Esto Photographics

129 Laviada House
Photo: Undine Prohl

130–131 Vancouver House, Vancouver, BC
Photos: Paul Warchol

132–133 Mountain Retreat, Park City, UT
Photos: Nic Lehoux

134 F-2 House, Mexico City, Mexico
Photo: Undine Prohl

135 *The White Box*, Tokyo, Japan
Photo: Toshihiro Komatsu

136 Tubac House, Tubac, AZ
Photo: Bill Timmerman

137 Guggenheim Museum, Las Vegas, NV
Photo: Michael Moran

138 Catalina House, Tucson, AZ
Photo: Wayne Fuji

139 Catalina House, Tucson, AZ
Photo: Bill Timmerman

144 Author photograph: Russell Baur

Index

Page numbers in *italics* refer to captions

Aalto, Alvar 95
Adria, Broid and Rojkind *90, 135*
Apple Store, North Michigan Avenue, Chicago *63*
Apple Store, Soho, New York *63*
architecture 8, 10, 20–1
Arima, Hiroyuki *65, 75, 122, 125*
Arizona State University, Tempe, Arizona *113*
Arts International HQ, New York *33, 70, 121*

Berman, Andrew *95, 96*
Bohlin Cywinski Jackson *47, 63, 65, 133*
Bohlin Residence, Waverly, Pennsylvania *47*
Boullé, Etienne-Louis 20–1
BR House, Araras, Brazil *84, 87, 127*

Cage, John 16–17, 140
Catalina House, Tucson, Arizona *86, 138, 139*
Cathedral of Our Lady of the Angels, Los Angeles *100*
Chapel of St. Ignatius, Seattle, Washington *6*
color 8–10, 12, 13, 16, *99, 118, 121*

Deaton, Charles *55*
Deaton House, Denver, Colorado *55*
DelMonico/Washburn Residence, New York *70*
Dominus Winery, Yountville, California *108*
Duchamp, Marcel 8, 60, 80

Einstein, Albert 8, 19

F-2 House, Mexico City, Mexico *90, 135*
Flavin, Dan 12–13, 140
Forest House, Connecticut *65*
form 21
400 Rubio Avenue, Tucson, Arizona *45, 75*

Gabellini, Michael
 form *57*
 glass *61, 67*
 lines of light *34, 36, 37, 38*
 windows *80, 83*
Giovannini, Joseph *49, 50, 53, 100*
glass 21 *see also* skylights; windows
Gluckman, Richard 18–19
Greenberg House, Los Angeles *104, 115, 117*
Guggenheim Museum, Las Vegas *137*

Hanrahan Meyers 8, 140–1
 color *22, 24, 27, 28, 29, 33, 121*
 glass *67, 68, 70, 72, 73, 77, 78*
 reflections *121, 128*
 windows *83, 92*
Hau, Lene 8, 14–15, 140
Herzog and DeMeuron *108*
Holley Residence, New York *73*
Holley House, Garrison, New York *92–93*
Hotel Habita, Mexico City, Mexico *80*

IL Kim *89, 97, 135*

Jil Sander Worldwide Showroom, Milan *34, 36, 37, 38, 39, 80*
Jones, E. Fay *107, 113*
Joy, Rick *45, 46, 75, 86, 106, 137, 138, 139*

Kalach and Alvarez *45*
Kogan, Marcio *84, 87, 127*
Koolhaas, Rem *137*

Laviada House, Mexico *128*
Layer House, Kobe, Japan *41, 43*
Le Corbusier 34, 80
Legorreta, Ricardo *104, 115, 117, 128*
light art 11–14, 48, *53, 55,* 60, 80
lines of light 20, 21
Lupo, Frank *61*

Michelangelo 48
Mies van der Rohe, Ludwig 21, 118
Moneo, Raphael *100*
Mountain Retreat, Park City, Utah *133*
music 15–18, 19

Naito, Rei *12,* 13–14, 141
National Gallery of Canada, Ottawa *110, 111*
Nicholson Garden Room, London *85*

Ohtani, Hiroaki *41, 43*
Olympic Tower Residence, New York *61, 83*

Part, Arvo 12, 15–16, 141
Patkau Architects *131*
Pawson, John *35, 90*
Pima Canyon House, Tucson, Arizona *46, 106*
Predock, Antoine *113*

Red Hook Center for the Arts, Brooklyn, New York *22, 24*
reflection 10–11, *22, 29, 33*
Richardson, H.H. 118
Rowan, Daniel *61*

Safdie, Moshe *110, 111*
Sarphatistraat Offices, Amsterdam *31, 99, 118*
Schrom Television Studios, Queens, New York *27, 28, 29, 33, 72*
Second Plate House, Fukuoka, Japan *65, 75, 122, 125*
785 Park Avenue Residence, New York *67*
shadow 11, *41*
Simmons Hall, MIT, Cambridge, MA *55, 57, 59, 102, 103, 121*
Simon Conder Associates *85*
Singer Residence, East Hampton, New York *128*
666 House, Mexico *45*
skylights 20, *22, 27, 41, 110, 111, 113, 131*
speed of light 8, 14–15
Steven Holl Architects *6*
 color *31, 118*
 form *55, 57, 59*
 reflections *118, 121*
 skylights *99, 102, 103*

Temple, Mary 8, *12,* 14
TEN Arquitectos *80*
theater 18–19
Thorncrown Chapel, Eureka Springs *107, 113*
Tubac House, Tubac, Arizona *137*

Urban Fourth *65, 75, 122, 125*

Vancouver House, Vancouver *131*
video art 10–11
Viola, Bill 10–11, 141
Vitiello, Stephen 17–18, 141

Walsh House, Telluride, Colorado *35, 90*
water 118, *122, 125, 127, 128, 131, 133, 135*
White Apartment, New York *61*
White Box, Tokyo *89, 97, 135*
White Space, New York *67, 68, 77, 78, 83*
Whitespace Studios, New York *95, 96*
Wilson, Robert 18–19, 141
windows 14, 20, *31,* 60, *77*
Wright, Frank Lloyd 118

hMa and Victoria Meyers

New York architects Victoria Meyers and Thomas Hanrahan believe that architecture is an environment, 'pure space', manifested in nature. The principals of Hanrahan Meyers Architects (hMa) have established themselves as unique visionaries, incorporating light and sound into their arresting designs of pure forms. Founded in 1987, the firm specializes in residences, art centers, and community spaces. They design spaces from a vision that connects visitors in unique conversations with the natural world. The firm has been recognized internationally with awards, publications, and exhibitions. Currently, **hMa** has projects under construction including WaveLine Performance Center in Queens, New York; Holley House in Garrison, New York; Pratt Design Center, Brooklyn, New York; Tenth Church of Christ Scientist in New York; and Ojai Performance Pavilion, Ojai, California. **hMa**'s community center at Battery Park City's North Neighborhood is adjacent to Ground Zero. This project is being designed as a LEEDS certified building, incorporating state-of-the-art lighting and solar technologies as key elements of the design. In 2003 **hMa** were invited to participate in the international development of houses in Sagaponac, New York, published by Rizzoli in *The Houses at Sagaponac*. **hMa**'s residential work was featured in *The Un-Private House* exhibition mounted at the Museum of Modern Art in New York in 1999. **hMa** has received awards from *Progressive Architecture* magazine, AIA NY Chapter, *Architectural Record* magazine, and from MIT they received the Eugene McDermott Award for Outstanding Design Talent. **hMa**'s work has been featured at the Museum of Modern Art, and published in *Architecture, Architectural Record, Domus, Lofts, The New American Apartment, GA Houses, DBZ Magazine, A + U,* and *Harper's Bazaar.*

In 2002 **hMa** published *The Four States of Architecture*, with Wiley and Sons. **hMa**'s interest in light and sound extends beyond the design of the performance spaces to the creation of the art itself. In the summer of 2004, the firm was selected from an international field of architects to design a 'light score' in collaboration with composer Michael Schumacher. This piece was performed at The Kitchen in New York as part of a summer-long festival entitled 'New Sounds New York'. In a current project the firm is designing an anamorphic, sculptural wooden box to house computer equipment for sound installations by various New York composers. The Music Box was commissioned by Schumacher, with whom the firm has an ongoing working relationship.

Victoria Meyers is a founding partner at **hMa**. She has been principal on a number of award winning projects in the firm, including Holley House, Red Hook Center for the Arts, Marfa Theater, Schrom Studios, Arts International, Sagaponac House, and Ojai Festival Performance Shell. In addition to numerous public projects, Ms. Meyers works with residential clients on award winning houses, loft apartments, and furniture. In 2004 she was featured as one of twelve **'Wonder Women'** at ICFF in New York. Ms. Meyers works closely with several galleries and assists private clients and galleries with the design of spaces for contemporary art collections. In 2004 she was invited to design a 'light score' as part of the Kitchen's celebration of *New Sound New York: Architects design music.* Ms. Meyers received her M.Arch from Harvard and an A.B. in Art History and Civil Engineering from Lafayette College.
She has taught at Columbia University Graduate School of Architecture and Planning, New York; City University, New York; Pratt Institute, New York; and Cornell University, Ithaca. Ms. Meyers has been awarded grants from the New York Foundation for the Arts and the Graham Foundation.

Websites featuring the work of Hanrahan Meyers Architects:
www.hanrahanMeyers.com
www.victoriameyers.com
www.hMa-home.com

There is also a website devoted to this book: www.designingwithlight.us